ONE WAY TO ASK

Poems by Daniel Ari

ONE WAY TO ASK

Poems by Daniel Ari

NORFOLK PRESS

ONE WAY TO ASK

Poems by Daniel Ari

with art by

Chuck H. Alston
Carole Ambauen
Sybil Archibald
Daniel Ari
Lauren Ari
Mirabai Ari
Carol Aust
Mark Bell
Stefan G. Bucher
Marna Scooter Cascadia
Jeannine Chappell
Roz Chast
R. Crumb
Veronica de Jesus
Henrik Drescher
Joakim Drescher
Gitty Duncan
Lauren Elder
Reza Farazmand
David Fleischmann
Michael Fleischmann
John Yoyogi Fortes
Tom Franco
Sheila Ghidini
Regina Gilligan
Andrew Goldfarb
Arthur Gonzalez
Roberta Gregory
Bill Griffith
Mark Hammermeister
Elizabeth Hird
Katina Huston
Kato Jaworski
Matt Jones

Chamisa Kellogg
Joe Kowalczyk
Ines Kramer
Krystine Kryttre
Eric Lindsey
Liz Maxwell
Angelin Miller
Tony Millionaire
Doug Minkler
Art Moura
Jay Musler
Allan Peterson
Aisha Rahim
Shraya Rajbhandary
Dianne Romaine
Christian Roman
Cybele Rowe
Janice Sandeen
Shiori Shimomura
Joyce Shon
Tony Speirs
Bob Stang
Livia Stein
Chip Sullivan
Rachell Sumpter
Kyle Trujillo
Jon Turner
Kerry Vander Meer
Ben Walker
Jerad Walker
Matt Weatherford
Wayne White
Heather Wilcoxon
Derek Wilson

Published by
Norfolk Press
398 11th Street, 2nd Floor
San Francisco, CA 94103
www.norfolkpress.com

Cover artwork and design by Eric Lindsey.
Cover photo by Lauren Ari.
Book design by Stefan G. Bucher for 344design.com.

1st Edition softcover

ISBN 978-1-60052-124-9

Printed in the United States of America.

Paper
Cover: Curious Metallics Anodized
Endsheet: Carnival Red Vellum
Text: Environment Irish Creme

Recycled post consumer fiber

FSC certified

100% Green-e certified

Carbon Neutral Plus

PCF Process Chlorine Free

Price: $35 USD

TO WONDER WOMAN

"We don't deserve resolution;
we deserve something better than that."
— Pema Chödrön

ONE WAY TO ASK

Introducing the Queron and *One Way to Ask*

"One way" with art by LAUREN ELDER

I

Can mind just be

mind running amuck?

II

ym dog is in her

bed   I see her

and I look at her

III

ask me whether
what I have done is my life.

IV

what difference between trees
and breakers?

V

Not even
the silence pursues me.

VI

In North America time stumbles on
without moving

INTRODUCING THE QUERON AND *ONE WAY TO ASK*

Queron is a form that emerged from my poetry practice to match the way my creativity dances, curiously and deliberately, with my experience. Querons have seventeen lines grouped into three quintets and a final couplet. The rhyme scheme is **ababa bcbca cdcdb dd.** I prefer subtle rhyme.

Querons have intentional line length, which means that the number of syllables— or accents or words—follows some conscious pattern.

The name *queron* evolved from the root of *query* and *querent* (the one for whom a tarot reading is done) to go with the sense of questioning, wonder, unknowing or awe that is an essential, broad element of the queron form. You can read more about querons in the long "introduction" at the end of this book.

I'm excited that other poets have started to write querons, and I certainly encourage you to try your hand at it. If you arrive at something you like, send it to me. My email is efflux@sonic.net, or you can post your poem as a comment at fightswithpoems. blogspot.com, or reach me through Norfolk Press (norfolkpress.com).

Collaborating with artists in making *One Way to Ask* has been hugely inspirational for me. The relationship between art and language is powerful and mysterious, creating a deepening of meaning and interest greater than a mere summing of parts. For more about the collaborative process and the artists, see the pages at the end of this book.

It makes me smile to imagine you reading in a comfortable place, taking your time, scanning the poems and art slowly, reading out loud, and reading again. Enjoy!

Daniel Ari
San Francisco, 2016

ONE WAY

Learning how to ask. The train pushes birds
into thundershower noise, a clapping
chorus, an old typewriter setting words.
They figure eights—hundreds of wings chopping
air. I think clouds. I think of the condors.

To practice asking is like sculpting smoke.
You have to keep giving up the figure.
Threads of the material keep tripping
your cough reflex, blowing your work to air.
You have to soften where hard luck frays you.

I have my first manual typewriter
in the garden. The earth helps it dissolve.
Last I saw a weedy euphorbia
has grown up through the chassis. We're absolved
for all the dancing and tapping we've done.

Experience as solvent. The great page
keeps evolving the tell beyond our tools.

"HANDS" by LAUREN ELDER

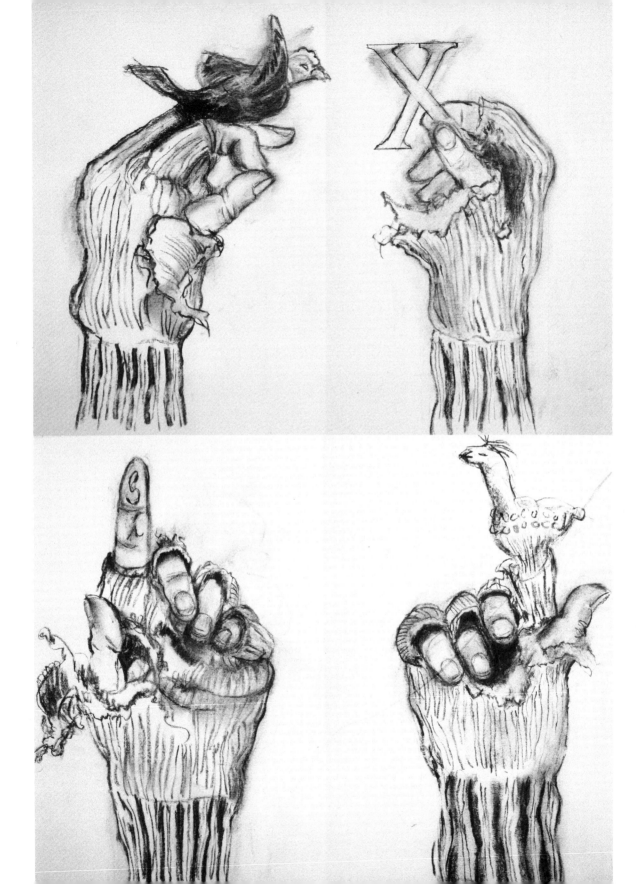

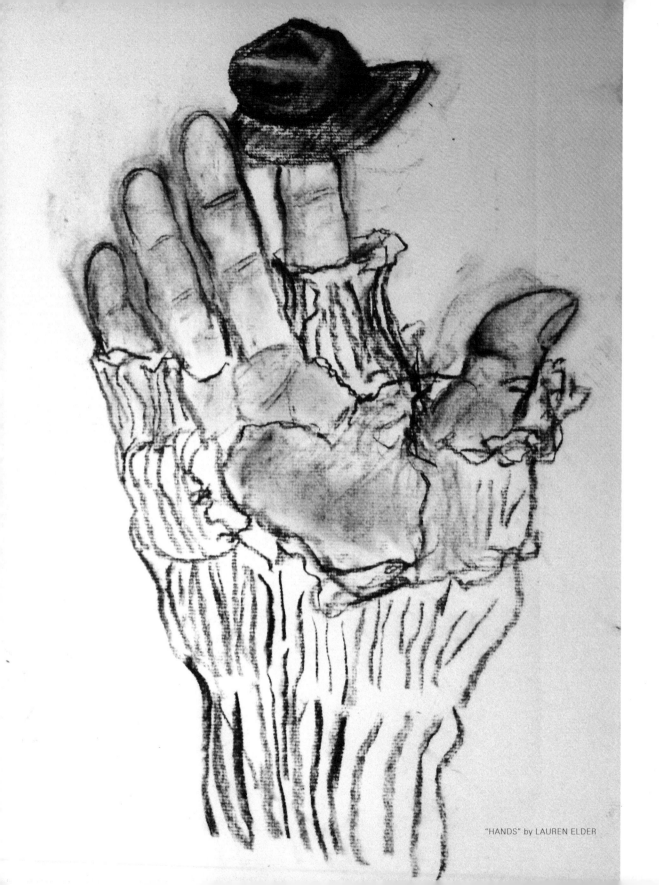

"HANDS" by LAUREN ELDER

CAN MIND JUST BE

MIND RUNNING AMUCK?

JANICE SANDEEN

DAVID FLEISCHMANN

ENGINEERED FURNISHINGS

In case the poetry thing doesn't work out
for me, you'll be relieved to know I have skills.
I build bookshelves, dressers, closets, cabinets,
and other furniture from prefab pieces.
I am a craftsman of only the finest

particle boards and composites. I have tools,
the complete set: a hammer, and not one but
two screwdrivers. I've also amassed some screws
and several Allen wrenches, now safely kept
behind the dryer. (If I need them, I'll get

a magnet and string.) I can read image charts
more or less, and build a Scandihoovian
credenza in fewer than four oh-fuck-its.
If I start at sunrise, by late afternoon
I'll have a new shelf and a couple BandAids.

Friends will come over and remark on the new
situation: "How's your poetry doing?"

HYOOMÄN

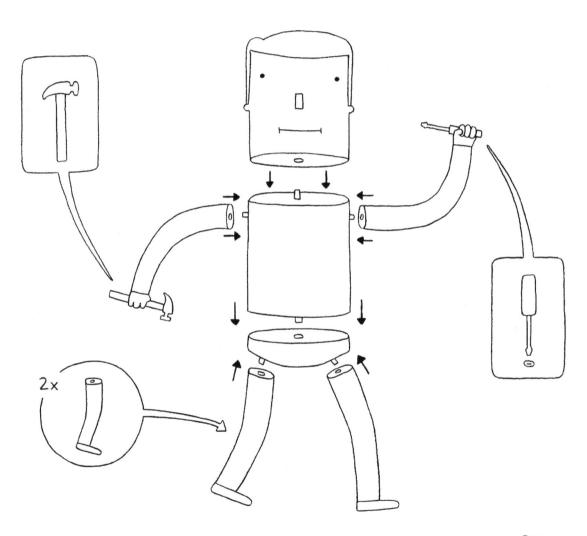

REZA

MISERY MOJO AND THE MINDS LESS BLOWN

> *"I'm a wearer of the dark.*
> *I'm a wearer of the dark.*
> *(I have a dark suit.)"*
> —*Dave Thomas*

Despite the bolt-rattling oscillation
of our heads, some of us punks were able
to half-wonder what would become of us
once the guitar's itch was scratched. "No Future"
begs certain questions in the aftershocks.

Crocus Behemoth blew our minds often,
mad head warbling like a climaxing teen;
but better than those sound-scrapes, his bitter
perspective diagonally conveyed
how frankly fucking smart we were, we punks.

But bands break. A car crash stopped D. Boon's jam.
Pop culture punks bit the dust on drugs (yawn)
while aging bassists coupled and had kids,
went to sew the sutures of middle age…
Crocus took up the accordion, whined

on about himself, wheezing through his art
and the girlfriends that came and went with it.

all You human beings look a lot alike to me

BAD IDEAS

Paul used to say—like when I suggested
going up to the G sharp and ending
the song there—never returning to D—
he'd crash the cymbal and cry, "Bad thinking—
let's try it!" One advantage of our band

aligning itself with Dadaism
was how experiments tended to stick
around, fermenting into pearlescent,
ginger liqueur that could thrill or sicken
audiences. My squeezebox case is closed

these days, and my creative output picked
into mostly harmless execution.
It's been years since I grabbed a trout and whacked
it against piano keys in passions
of Art. The cleaning staff hasn't minded,

at least, that I've gotten less splashy in
making forms from my itchy dissonance.
I can still smell the fish-sauced piano,
hear the few strange cries from the audience
and feel my rough breath in the stark silence.

Did we prove any point? I'm convinced that
our scales still have a more fluid balance.

MY GREAT AMERICAN NOVEL

I prayed that the friction of spinning wheels
would suffice to ignite the inferno—
prayed until bike tires turned to radials
skidding disharmony to radio
rock 'n' roll—until parked, cliff-edged, the squeals

of oceans, private boiling wet windows—
saw spark touch gas. The world began—at last—
to burn. Vesuvius blew. Phoenix rose.
Summer chased spring deep into parching grass.
They wove garlands for innocent impulse.

So soon cries of fruition—came so fast—
a tiny apple, an ember burning
to emerge, new fuel grown from the ashes—
searing to flourish, flush with the yearning,
children spark-throwing as my embers glow.

Shared concentration of heat returning,
this sustaining smolder of my learning.

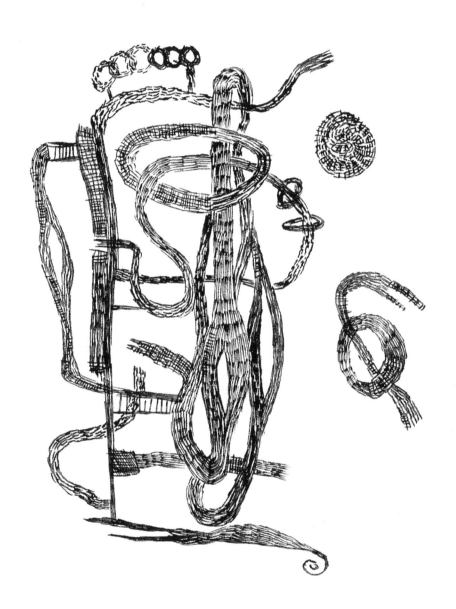

FIRST AND LAST STAND

I had an Armageddon dream. The godawful
explosion nearby sent its heat-maddened shrapnel
scudding from a cloud like a decorative bottle.
City center transformed into a great candle.
Then the mind's innate drive toward its own survival

shifted the dream's setting into a new panel.
In that setting, I was recording the prior
end-of-days scenario into my journal.
This dreamself explored the symbology of fire
in futures untouched by the Ragnarök fractal.

In the latter dream, I told you of the terror
we felt standing in the hot hail of the world's fall,
now passed into the safe angst of a dream's prior
dream; but your face fell, and fell away, the final
bell of the morning's first alarm. I want to call

life a blessing, shadows and all. But today, you'll
please allow me your soft voice and a tender smile.

HOLD FAST, HOLD FAST

How can I save the pieces
when more pieces keep falling
off? Times like these, I'm a sea-
eaten clipper in a squall.
Hatten down the batches! Please,

sea, see me to safe landfall.
Ropes and riders rattle, drop
off to dissolve on the calm
floor. Why shouldn't this whole ship
of self descend into peace?

Then all my pieces could sleep
where they rest, in one black bed
where slow, deep monsters would keep
me together, at last rid
of this wearing need to sail.

But then the ocean goes dead.
I think there's a shore ahead.

FOR THE FUZZ

Now that it's refused me, I'll refuse hair—
that's how I decided twelve years ago
to strip my head razor-clear and take air,
snow and sight without the diplomacy
of coiffure. Know my mind, world: it is here!

Since the divorce, my 'do has kept a low
profile, though I spot it on the fringes
at times. It has never regained the glow
it had when my follicles were engines,
the sex machines of our honeymoon years.

With fine gray fuzz, I sometimes get twinges
when I see some full-headed guy, recall
how at Burning Man, I stained it orange.
At twenty-two, I pulled a ponytail.
How could I have ever cursed you, Jewfro?

I was young and could complain my gall out
without recognizing there'd be fall out.

DAVID FLEISCHMANN

FREERADICAL2013

ROAD NOT TAKEN

I found myself once in a frosty wood
well equipped for the adventure but stopped
where the trail forked north and south. I stood there
looking up one path and its opposite,
sucking my canteen, thinking how I could

drink them both without a doppelganger.
Calling out overhead, a raven passed.
The worn trail had its opportunities;
instead, I followed her flight, climbing east
through pristine forest. The hood of the sky

drew down over me and my choices.
                                        Fast-
forward years from the day when I diverged,
and I'm at home. My toddler daughter must
slumber, leaving me to my craft of words,
a golden practice that earns some copper.

I've grown glad to consider myself weird.
She pads to the study and squeaks, "I'm scared."

"LEAVE NO TRACE" by CHUCK H. ALSTON

PARTLY PAVED

Where the road stopped, an old train track,
half-lost, crossed my trail's T. One way
pointed into town. It struck me
that I'd noticed the brown steel paved
into 3rd Street, the lot at Jack's,

and many spots where the railway
ran before the brambles of town
grew on it. The opposite ray
of vanishing track bent around
an overgrown, unbuilt hillock.

I went that way. Threadbare green gowns,
dappled silences, and a dry,
fickle creek filled the afternoon
until evening. Until the ties
stopped their ladder steps where I'd strayed.

Were they different, the northern skies
those days when coffee cost a dime?

DIAPHANY

The architecture of my dreams: hallways
in red velvet, broad as betting parlors,
spaces that signal transition—always—
and sometimes I come to a cellar door
that opens into a dark earthen maze.

It's familiar but not particular.
I begin squeezing down the labyrinth
until it's as wide as I. Yellow earth.
Unease rises. I crouch. Ahead: the depth.
I know the secret—I've known all my days!

I backtrack from the anonymous earth,
shut the basement door, return to the hall.
Hors d'oeuvres. The opera. No way to assert
what was where I went. Must wake to recall
the dark, the door, the essence I forget.

Through that grave, I wonder if there's a caul
a curtain drawn like nothing before all.

LOSE YOURSELF TO DANCE

and to Susana Baca

I find a point where I stop vanishing,
where all I am is breath, fluid, and meat,
and the substance between doesn't constrain.
I am only endlessly twirling sweat.
I've dropped away from some cloud of meaning,

a drop of music for the ground to eat.
Someday and starting now, I don't vanish
because all that's here is weight, sound and heat
in a moving mirage of human-shaped
container that sets the world spinning.

The sound of one hand clapping and the splash
of trees toppling in a distant forest:
the beat's complex; the lyrics are Spanish.
The mountain is moving inside my chest.
Saca la mano! Saca los pies!

Saca la cadera si te quieres
aprender—lost and found in whirling Yes.

"MOVEMENT AND BREATH" by ELIZABETH HIRD

CASTING

Months after moving in,
I was still new in town.
On any unassigned
weekday, cast on my own,
I'd ride N to the end,

west to the turnaround.
Singles dotted the sand.
I found my place and frowned.
Red beach blankets bannered
personals for women

and men, lovers or friends.
I'd discretely get stoned
and pretend to pretend
I wished to bathe alone.
At home, I would come down,

eat some soup, write a poem,
try to coax the unknown.

BREAK AT TOUCH

More than once my wife reenacted
our daughter's breaking water in tides
of tears and unheld urine. I held
steady, mostly; but on Friday nights
I put them to bed early and danced.

Flow chopped to staccato, frothed to flights
of chaos and blessed my wet father
body well beyond words. Two allies
emerged from rhythms, motion and sweat
to lay their hands on me. And they laid

my life out like a saturated
diaper, and like my infant daughter
I bawled for loss and cold discomfort
and for my wife who never thought her
life could crumble yet hold her alive.

We'd become flotsam in big water,
surprised fish flopping on a dance floor.

AN UNLIKELY STORY

Could I dismantle my stake in progress?
Delete a few of the novelty apps
from my iPhone? Stop using GPS?
Postpone texting while I'm on the crapper?
Can I leave the net, go mobilephoneless?

Can I store a dead laptop in burlap?
Without my computer, will there be lunch?
I'll work at home, schedule a midday nap.
I'll free the old well and muck out the sludge.
I will be thirsty. I will be a mess.

Where can I walk when the Honda won't budge?
Can I rest long nights in February?
I'll make my own music on wires and jugs.
I'll stitch my own wounds, meet pain's ecstasies,
and make a storied storehouse of my lap.

In summer only I'd eat ripe cherries,
and hang The Apple back upon The Tree.

KATO JAWORSKI

LETTER

(ABOUT A. D. 350)

LIGHT COMPLAINTS

I kvetch plenty —
except when you
ask me to; then
looking for blue,
I find cyan.

Kalamazoo
ain't Calcutta.
Work's a zoo, but
lunch is butter.
I can't complain.

A subtle shift
from unease and
mumblemutter
to unframed peace —
om babaloo.

So ask me, please,
sometimes to grouse.

YM DOg iS m her
bed I See her
and I Look at her
She iS CNte
yes She iS!

||

YM DOG IS IN HER

BED   I SEE HER

AND I LOOK AT HER

JOYCE SHON AND JAMES B. WHEELER

WE AGREE

for L

Bring our wedding cake topper onto The Antique Road Show.
The expert will turn it on a felt-topped folding table
with restrained enthusiasm about its monogram,
filigree, pedigree and, at last, its *je ne sais quoi.*
Though we're amateurs, the verdict's dramatic: Best In Show.

Yes, look at us now: in bed watching TV on a Tuesday,
adrift in tea, blankets and the broad seas of regular
passing among office, practice and kindergarten days.
Far from the wedding where we wept our joy, we land weary
with few words some nights, some nights a slight furrow in the brow.

The patina deepens on the worthy thing we have here
in the flats and troughs equally as in the barnburners
and breakers. By now we know we'll look, and it will appear
on the altar where we tend to it, sprouted and burnished,
ever the bright prize we seized together before the gray.

Under its still, resounding presence, think of all we've borne.
It's always here, dear, our golden little tabernacle.

WAYS TO THIS MAN'S HEART

Days I come up, a sun in conjunction
with satellites in a Milky Way bed.
If I'm the sun, they're the reasons to shine.
My atomic burning glows reflected
in a planetary constellation

of woman's, daughter's and terrier's heads.
And some tidal nights, I rise like a moon
to flash the broad desert of my forehead,
waning, looking forward to setting soon.
Astronomy motion steers my passions.

Our heavenly house orbits to open,
my love. Can you imagine we are spheres
talking lip to lip, swaddled in afghans
of nebulae, wormholes and star clusters?
Even infinity's vacuum is held.

Back in clodhoppers, your song takes my ears.
Our earth-bound heavens move my light light-years.

"COUNTERPART #6" by KERRY VANDER MEER

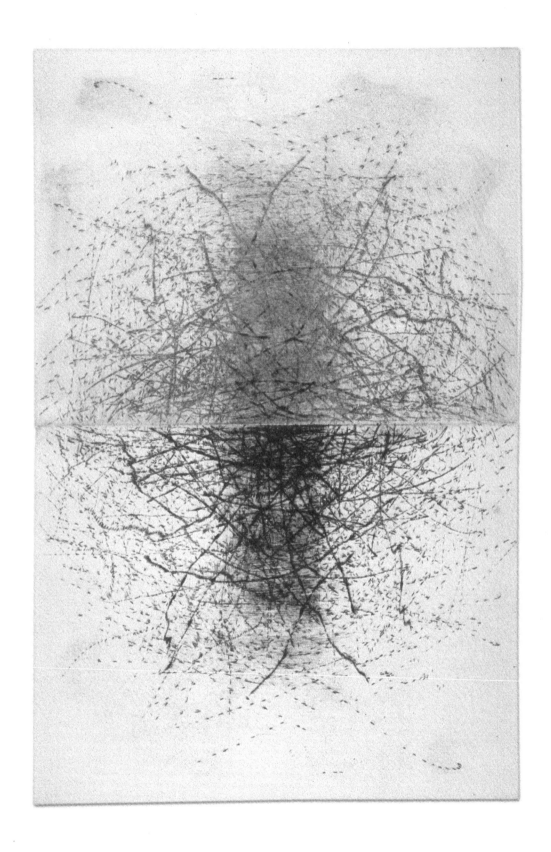

PLUM SEASON

We walk slowly by each plum tree
asking the maroon camouflage
for its few pieces of ruby.
I steady and leap to dislodge
any I see for you or me.

This is the season of the hajj.
We make it as a fruitful prayer
to pick our place in the collage,
so take the lively Asian pear,
kumquat, kiwi, huckleberry.

Swallowing sugar, we compare
this year with prior ones and spit
seeds all the way to paradise.
The path is fertile with the pits.
We slurp the seasons, every age

balled up into these wild, bitter-
sweet fruits we feel lucky to eat.

THE FALLOW MONTHS

My hunger, love, is like an alien moon.
I know you feel its phases subtly
as tired nights pale from busy afternoons.
The strange globe with its aching liquid pull—
astronomical and inopportune—

has stirred storm clouds lately, love. It grows full
and stirs tides and winds into two hoarse cries.
In here, we've battened down, sorted the mail.
Do you remember the last time that eye
closed in satisfied rest in the cocoon,

turbulence muted under the duvet
of earth's shadow? Did you know sixty-two
moons (nine of them provisional) fly by
Saturn, not to mention the rings? And do
you know how insistent my orbital

gravity winds up? Even typhoons blow!
You're the sovereign sea, but I'm thirsty, too.

"ASTRONOMICAL & INOPPORTUNE" by DANIEL ARI

HOUSE GUEST

Gasses wrapped her from the inside;
building materials sealed her.
The doorstep evicted the bride.
Her homing heart could not find where
any room in there still opened.

She sat on the curb. A neighbor
came whose own heart bled quite enough,
who said, "Well, what's a great room for?
The Big One doesn't make us tough.
It just rattles off our pride. Come."

On the sofa, she slept and sloughed
the cellophane ribbons and chains.
She dreamed about her nephew who
had not resurfaced from the strain.
At last, one clear afternoon tore

the seal open, and out she came—
wet, trembling, beginning again.

FOR RICHARDSON BAY

I'm going to walk the next part of my path
farther from you, I'm sad to say. It's not
my choice. There's good in it, but I'd rather
stay near. While I surge in and out on BART,
you'll keep languishing in your endless bath.

Some extraordinary day when it's hot—
it may be years from now—I'll come across
the bridges to walk with you and visit
about those days and these days. Eight years passed
in your embrace, breathing your marshy breath.

When summer comes, how will I not miss you
in the city with all its distractions?
Union Square swamps with shoppers and tourists
making each day's commercial commotion,
but there may be days or weeks I forget

the surge and suck of water in motion
though so close the bay kisses the ocean.

"MEMORY BAY" by INES KRAMER

FORTUNE'S CASTLE

I've so many
good wishes from
Chinese cookies
saved in my home,
you'd think to see

diamonds and plums
in Chihuly
bowls in each room.
But actually,
bowls by Ari

fill with pennies
and small apples
from our own tree.
Fortune's simple
sugary crumbs

fill my temple.
My luck's ample.

IN-LAW UNCLE MARK

I felt you never felt the need to talk
just to talk. You talked about the weather,
the food, and common sense on the slow walk
up the boardwalk to Salty's Seaside where
my daughter entertained us all, gawking

at the gulls on the railing, the lobsters
in the tank, the sweet shop across the pier—
your silent amusement, a comfort. Your
sisters, wife and nieces cheerfully gabbed.
You didn't drink, having sold alcohol.

You stocked the parties, worked on New Year's Eve.
I think you'd smile to know your wife whooped me
in online Scrabble yesterday. The word
PASTIME cinched her 90-point victory.
Your grandson loved playing with my daughter.

They hid and sought at the winery where,
finally married, your son looked so happy.

DON'T FORGET IT (WITH CURLY WEAVER)

Teenagers on the public playground set
in crawlplace shadows tight enough for two.
                (Whatcha gonna do? How 'bout you?)
The sky's gone dark; and as it's getting wet,
bodies too big for slides find something new.
                (I dare you to. I dare you, too.)

The time comes fast—not yet—to go—not yet!
Press and promise, Beth, one last taste of you,
                of you, Beth, one more taste of you
before we climb out of the jungle gym,
and walk you home by the light of the moon—
                the ba-ding-a-dong-ding blue moon.

The moon has waned and waxed three hundred times
since the last shadow-heated time we met,
                that last time on the playground set.
While I'm certain I could find you online,
who I'd find… well, I wouldn't make a bet
                she'd be she from that tête-à-tête.

Beth, I hardly ever hear you calling.
My emotions aren't a marionette,
                no longer my hormones' puppet.
But some foggy fragrance just brought me to
that feeling I knew I'd never forget
                (or if I will, I haven't yet).

Teenagers on a public playground set.

"PLAYGROUND" by ROBERTA GREGORY

-15- Roberta Gregory

SWEET BOY, THOUGH CERTAINLY NO ROMEO

—as Judy C.

Advantages to living on a thoroughfare:
1. You never have to make a map. 2. You can
always entertain guests just by taking them for
a walk through your own famous neighborhood. 3. When
he comes over, you can talk about the street fair.

Disadvantages: Parking is the biggest one.
You agreed on eightish and it's past nine. He could
be circling the blocks, or he could have forgotten
or decided to do something else. But wouldn't
he call? I wonder if I should light the fireplace.

At last! He comes in, skin flushed, bringing me a good
apology for his adventures in parking.
My roommate left a half bottle of Ravenswood.
We work on that, talking about the fair, talking
as his flush actually deepens. Though I didn't

light the fire, he says he's hot and starts removing
layers. Suddenly the scientist, I'm watching.

THE RABBI'S DAUGHTER

In the Torah story,
the way I pictured it,
the nude woman simply
took Adam by the bits
and led him to the tree…

Beth smiled. She had grown tits
and talked like she had plans
with me. Zeda witnessed
the scene. When she moved on
alone, he said, "You're slow."

I couldn't imagine
how we'd go from shmoozing
to a private Eden,
just the new, naked two
of us, clicking magnets

from, "Hi. How do you do?"
to the biblical zoo.

"I LIKE YOUR HAT," HE OPENED.

"Voo nur a meshuggener, khapn sich tzu mir." —*Yiddish saying*
(*Crazy people always grab onto me.*)

"Keep this a secret," he said. "Matt Damon
wants to produce my life story himself—
but that's not why I quit." He touched my hand.
"I was the co-owner of Yelp.com."
The train was packed; also I was spellbound

not with calculating his mental health
(in two dull seconds), but how we travelled
a genre storyline now. Elf king caught
on a quest, needing his future foretold;
and me, the oracle, for I happened

along, at first a maybe-one-night stand
but soon a secret compassion sharer.
We held council until my commute's end.
I hugged him bye by the escalator;
the crowd surged, and I saw him take the lift

to the inbound platform, there to search for
another hat. A seer. Two new ears.

HOLD THAT TIME

"Meet me in St. Louis, Louis…"
if my seven-year-old daughter
were a U.S. year, she would be
1947. Summer.
While the movie's a slog to me,

she is transported on Garland's
Technicolor eyes to a time
cradled tenderly in the arms
of a later time that used film
as a salve. A bright opiate.

Maybe she won't find out how glum
Judy became. The plot's struggles,
in retrospect, are quick to dim.
When we watch the "Making of" reel,
it opens with clips of bombers.

Instead we go on Google to
The Fair and Liza Minnelli.

"JUDY GARLAND" by SHRAYA RAJBHANDARY

BABA, AN AMERICAN WOMAN

When my grandmother was dying
I asked her… I don't remember.
Such sparse decor. I'm wondering,
baba, can you say what you've learned?
Very old people sat watching

game shows. Baba was pretty far
gone already, prone to private
spirals of thought. We sat in chairs
at a round table. Two sedate
nurses counted pills. A bell rang

from the TV: some contestant
rewarded for a good answer?
She said, "America, a light
among nations…" Then she warbled,
"Israel."

       "Israel?"

              She turned

her head toward the picture window
filled with a seasonless color.

MUSICAL PINS

Which goofish songs should I sing to my offspring?
Which among the endless favorites do I frame
in fleeting windows of cultural training—
training, bo-baining, banana, fana fame?
The Ministry of Silly Walks. Ning Nang Nong.

Everything on YouTube is, in ways, the same.
Which silly songs will my offspring sing to me?
Will she loop It's Peanut Butter Jelly Time
behind some failed candidate's concession speech?
I dig it's a catchy spoof, though I'm aging

with the standards in my organ's memory.
To share is share enough! We have in common
maps, spots, sing-alongs, phrenological peaks.
LaVerne, Maxene, Patty and Lord Buckley bear
our closeness closer in true and skewed rhymes, so

Sing the Beer Barrel Polka, that peppy air,
or make something up over Scarborough Fair.

© Bill Griffith

MICKEY, WHO WAS A SOCIAL WORKER

Imagine The Three Stooges' Larry Fine,
the curly haired one, as a loveable
gentleman with enthusiastic eyes.
Even when I was a kid and babbling,
he'd look at me like the shiniest dime.

I can see the mensch now, unshakeable
in the fertile bedrock of family line—
and his seven kids, equally stable,
so that when I talked, they paid attention;
and when I grew I recognized the signs

of traditional Jewish compassion,
the transplant's sensed duty to share the bread.
Pre-nuclear family American
head of a larger household, wherein heads
put together put meals on the table—

food for the city, haven for each child.
Whatever I said, Uncle Mickey smiled.

"UNCLE MICKEY" by VERONICA DE JESUS

PUP'S OLD

Bella's imperturbable as she sleeps,
once the bursting free girl who chased the years,
balls, sticks, and frisbees, foaming meadow greens
until her muscles cramped, and her peaked ears
rounded, and her tongue pierced and pierced the breeze,

which always roves in when the sun covers
itself. Then in the play field's aftermath,
a walk home, a deposit scooped, suppers
all around, and everyone gets a bath.
(For some, that's a chance to earn a few treats.)

The eternal puppy exhales dog breath.
She mouths her stuffed squid, but won't tug a game.
She no longer levitates off the earth,
snapping for a toy or a bite of lamb.
The cold weather affects old Bella's knees.

She licks my face from a different timeframe,
and it smells like I'll never be the same.

JEANNINE CHAPPELL

TÓCAME

Inspired by Karl Frost

Anticipation butters my skin
like a hot skillet jumping garlic.
You're going to touch me and take me in.
How slowness makes our thoughts come so quick!
When our bodies meet—what will happen?

We cook a harmonious conflict:
Chillies strike. Honey blocks. Human tongues
penetrate time, licking the future
to the past, blending ingredients,
pushing the meat back to meet the bone.

Your shades were parted, and your windows
stood clear. Then, through my reflected face,
I saw your greenest wishes glinting.
You watched my shadow enter your space,
and smiled like a sublime heretic:

We're ready to slough the carapace
and let our whole bodies take the feast.

11

THE PIPES, THE PIPES ARE CALLING

He's on "Hello, Dolly" now, the dapper
busker whose honey baritone echoes
past the turnstiles, down the escalators
into the seats of the San Francisco
train—but it's you, my Danny Boy, who turned

my commute into sunshine and shadow—
how as I bustled into the station
his oboe voice rose and called "Oh, Danny
Boy"—how I stopped marching as he began
invoking *my name*, the song my father

sang to me on cassettes—and in person
when he came home from the war—how I stayed
to see him smile, to watch the lyrics sink
down the tiles, into the ground where the trains
rush their gears into the quick and the slow

day pretending to continue apace
while songs in ceaseless chorus play and play.

PAIR O' DICE FOUND

"All the way to heaven is heaven." —*Catherine of Siena*

It's not the casino's artless deco
or the band exhuming Grandmaster Flash.
It's the shaking mojo and letting go
of every last thing but one pointless wish:
Little Joe, Little Joe from Kokomo!

Communion wine cocktails have all but washed
my sins of riven attention away.
The choir forgets all about the cash
as the dice hover in gospel and sway,
fall, tumble and stay—two and two. That's four!

Hallelujahs rise not because six pays
twelve. Our bones rattle in the joker's house
as we pray for hard ways and easy ways
and watch each new present outcome degauss
question and answer. Our soul's heaven switch

flips, and we flip. That's what it's about: this
surrendering soul of the holy souse.

STARLIGHT COMPOST IS THE NAME SHE TOOK.

That woman looked like Dan'l Boone,
comfortable despite the swelter,
tan and tough as her buckskin suit.
When we asked, she said she found deer
road dead, balanced them on her bike,

and pedaled them toward better use.
You cut 'round the hooves, she explained,
and open up the viscera.
You soften the hide with the brains.
The deer's memory box is fat rind

you rub in to stain and strengthen
the leather. It'll resist cold,
tears and punctures. It'll shed rain.
It's a necessity, she said
and her eyes started to well up.

"Deerkind are so perfectly made
on the inside and the outside."

FAERIE PANIC

My kid emerges from her room in tears.
Figure it's another grumpy rising.
Muster pre-coffee patience for her flares.
Wonder what's the plot. Favorite socks missing?
Honey spread too thin? No, she's in despair—

her tooth—fuck me! Her front tooth was waiting
all night long for a distracted fairy.
No cash, not even a note this morning!
The resident spirits negligently
fell asleep entwined, their duties ignored.

She sobs into the shirt she pulls on. We
improvise desperately, stuffing singles
into a red sachet, calligraphy
sign, hot potato it to the fishbowl.
"Hey! What's that by the tank? Is something there?"

She comes, wipes her eyes, collects her windfall.
"Weird," she sniffs. "They didn't use my pillow."

♥ Tooth
Fairy

MORE FAERIE TRICKERY

Like pi, a weird magic between
whole numbers, tooth faeries wiggle.
My daughter's teeth hold new questions
we would have daubed with Orajel
while retelling the old legends.

Now I tell her my eyes are old
and can't see all I have the will
to believe. I work at the role
of faerie, and I feel dispelled
as she peels the irrational

details from our storybook world.
Soon she's sure to explore behind
the painted sets. Then she can tell
her own legends. For now, she's signed
another month's lease in that realm

where teeth pay the dear rents in kind
and one sprite outgrows his disguise.

EVENING ETUDE

Pink light comes inside with handshakes
or hugs, whichever you prefer.
It doesn't want soup. It just takes
a long look into the corners
of your face, noticing the ache.

It's a travelogue when mother's
on the phone—Greece and Italy,
book club, beach—like the adventures
you had in your Air Force family
moving to Hilo from Fort Knox.

You've come to summarize briefly
at the end of each call: "Love you."
"Love you, too." You hear what you mean.
You hang up and reheat the soup.
The pink light is heading westward.

It says it must. It says adieu
with a last gold glint. See you soon.

"CONVERSATION" by SHEILA GHIDINI, COURTESY OF CHANDRA CERRITO CONTEMPORARY

LAUREN ARI

III

ASK ME WHETHER
WHAT I HAVE DONE IS MY LIFE.

—WILLIAM STAFFORD

GITTY DUNCAN

WHO WEPT AT THE ROMANCE

for Ginsberg and so for Solomon

The moon yacketayakking
all over the street danced on
boxcars. Boxcars racketing
over the rooftops. Storefront
Moloch, whose ear is smoking,

wandered around and around
seeking jazz or sex or soup,
trying to giggle, but wound up
with a sob—animal soup
intelligent and shaking.

The archangel of the soul
will never return your soul,
faded out in vast sordid
movies. Holy Istanbul
vanished into nowhere Zen.

Midnight streetlight smalltown rain
ended fainting on the wall.

HEATHER WILCOXON

WHAT'S COOKING

My grandmother called this "Snare-a-husband."
She never wrote out the recipe but
made me memorize it before she died.
I'm humming the song of ingredients,
stirring around your name, my bowl, my bird.

Yet your freedom's what I love most, my heart,
and I'm far too giddy to bake a trap
even if I wanted to. When we part
tonight with our bellies full, night will wrap
its separate dreams around us. My David,

will you dream of me? Earthy smells rise up
layering the edible atmosphere
held steaming beneath the coal-crusted tarp
of stars. If you will be mine, then we're here
for that purpose. Eat, my friend. Fill your plate.

Two birds told me about the weight you bear.
Swallow that bite then share, please, share your thoughts.

AISHA RAHIM

2/16/92

HOW I MET YOUR FATHER

Goddess Mother knows I don't go to the hot springs
to hook up with anyone, least of all a guy.
He sat on the edge of the cold pool, gesturing
without a conversation. I got tingly thighs.
His lips whispered; his gaze flitted. A queer longing

came to blow out that clogged funnel of a man. Why?
He seemed naked—he was naked—but in a shell,
a veil of views painted on his personal sky.
Anyway, I'm sure it all comes down to our smells.
I got close enough to stop his eyes from spinning

and coaxed his story, which came in surges and swells.
When he asked mine, I closed my smile and sang, "If you
could read my mind, love, what a tale my thoughts would tell."
Lighthearted, Lightfooted, we watched the empty blue
catch stars. I understood he wished for empty eyes.

It's what a healer doesn't hesitate to do:
hone the attention, turn the clogged funnel and blow.

"EVERYTHING" by HENRIK DRESCHER

WHOSE IDEA?

"We send monkey out to Planet X in the Horsehead Nebula—
the planet that looks like it's coming and going at the same time—
so monkey can collect soil samples and watch the stars being born."
                                                    —Dan Carbone

Records that no one will ever review
reflect you were assembled once upon
a forfeited planet and placed into
a vast, indifferent deepness. Your controls
are dialed more toward "to be," less toward "to do."

The sea between no ties and notices
is one you cross without reckoning how
a far distant glint birthed a perception
that there may be something you're meant to know,
a new mission to be revealed to you.

But what it was that flashed is never shown.
When you arrive where you thought you would take
the source, undifferentiated glow
surrounds you. If you feel, then it's an ache.
You have to stop. You have to consider.

Your current programming may be a fluke.
With only your wiring, what can you make?

FEEDBACK ON 4.5

Carlton's grandson unwrapped a BB gun—
a real rifle with a real caliber.
"After breakfast I'll show you how it's done."
"Oh, boy!" Dad was blasé. Mom was angry.
"I thought we had an agreement, Carlton."

"It comes with safety lessons, don't worry,"
  he winked at the boy, "taught by the master."
"He's too young." "You're too protective, Debbie."
"Ralph?" She turned, but Dad was in another
  room, a vote in absentia.
                              "Not funny!"

yelled Carlton at the boy who'd said "Pweee!"
with the sight to his eye, aiming at Buck,
  the old retriever drowsing on the hearth.
"You are responsible for protecting
  your family and yourself." But his daughter,

when he glanced at her, looked livid. "Go back
to L.A.," she shot. "Have a heart attack."

MICHAEL FLEISCHMANN

CLASS ACTION SUIT: WOMEN V. SHAHRYAR

Dear sisters, your pussies were perfect.
Your amber-rose temples, each of them,
were jewels to make soldiers genuflect
and drop their swords to the sea's bottom.
But this dick? Who could have expected

he'd roll off livid post-orgasm?
It's not your fault you trusted your sex
to sway the tyrant from his tantrum.
But soon as I imagined the next
murder, I knew my aim was correct:

Use my throat, my upper tube, to vex
his violence one night at a time.
Now this throat arrests him and convicts,
sentences him and brings home the crime.
Repenting, he's at peace when it comes

three years later. He drifts into dream;
and then, for us all, I castrate him.

SOHAM WHAT I AM

Soham is Sanskrit for "I am That."

Some swabs you just can't satisfy
however you marshal your force.
The liar fells you with a lie.
The idler borrows hamburgers.
You tilt your hat forward to try

until trying becomes your course,
and victories define your qi,
and conflict draws your universe—
and then *to struggle* is *to be*.
One day I asked me: "What am I?"

One eye to see the one great sea.
One pipe to smoke the traveling sky.
One me without an enemy,
a mouthful of spinach close by.
I went to meet the Sea Hag—hers

the crone's wisdom, the typhoon's eye.
We mean at last to still the storm,
atone our fight. My soul sings aye.
To blow *myself* down—this I am—
seeking the Sea Queen's single peace.

Breathing the wet air—*ham soham*—
we're weaving from the warp a calm.

"WHAT I AM" by TONY SPEIRS

DISCHARGE

Sitting in the back of a Greyhound bus,
you find out who you are without orders.
Without family meeting you there to fuss,
you get dismissed last. At o dark thirty
you might sleep, but you can't, and there's no rush.

Two hundred miles to Brookings. Forty more
to Cairn Station, and then you walk a mile
to the house and whoever you find there,
strapped for cash, fast asleep and unable
to give you a hug, tell you where to toss

your reeking, desert-dusted duffel bag.
You drive to McDonalds, and then you give
the orders: Big Mac, Coke, side of Kabul.
You've choppered, jeeped, flown, bussed, walked and driven
for two all-beef patties in the free world.

And in the world, watertight as a sieve,
gonna have to figure out how to live.

"HAPPY U.S. MEAL" by DEREK WILSON

THAT GOOD OL' BOY WOULD NOT STAY DOWN

One summer three kids drowned
under Jotunheim Falls.
They warned, "Don't horse around.
The stream might look small, but
the force can shove you down."

In the spray, we always
watched where the water hit.
Sean, most coltish of all,
would swim up and tease it.
He made *us* the grown-ups.

One steaming day, Sean went
higher than our jump spot—
then higher—holy shit—
fetched the Paul Bunyan top—
and leapt. The wide world stalled.

Our earthbound hearts stopped. Stopped.
He was lost. Mist.

                            Then—pop!

"WATERFALL" by RACHELL SUMPTER

JUNGLE REVIVAL

Even after watching him smack face first
into countless trees over endless days,
the ape named Ape had still not fully guessed
the depths of his friend George's naiveté—
not until George's "Doggie," Shep traversed

the ancestral passage to the graveyard
of elephants. George continued calling
for Shep at dusk and setting out huge plates
of chow insisting he would be hungry
when he came home. George's mate, Ursula,

and Ape both tried to explain what dying
was; but George would open a breadfruit and
shout, "Here, Shep!" Ape was awed at the Living
Saint of Primal Innocence; he soon left
to live with his ape tribe. He was afraid

of seeing George laid on his own deathbed.
Meanwhile, George still swings, calling out for Shep.

SERIOUS INK

"Pinstriped skin? You want pinstriped skin?"
  So, naturally, you repeat it.
"Okay, okay. The Pinstripe Kid."
  He's old. He fetches his needles
  and a jar of powdered black ink.

"Take a couple months. At least weeks,
  you know." Yes, you know. The man slakes
  the ink from a cracking teapot.
  Though chilly, you take off your slacks.
"So what's up?" he asks. "You pissed off

  at your mother?" But when he asks,
  it's at the back wall, an aside.
  So you don't say anything. "Fuck,"
  he barks, laughs or coughs. *What?* "Hell. Stripes.
  You know? Never mind. You ready?"

You are. Each etching stroke feels like
bursting across a finish line.

CRAPPIEST PLACE ON EARTH

Indeed, we found rat turds in the kitchen.
Mickey and Minnie hosted a soirée.
We killed ten in May; they were back by June
while the Mars Café sold a hundred trays
of fries each day, cleansed in canola oil.

Just down from Journey Into Inner Space
was our rat hole, a door nobody saw.
We cussed in under-park tunnels, made days
magic for marks as un-mustachioed,
supporting cast. We'd sneak oral and waltz

to get paid, shuck the shit-suits and go home.
Some artist in the sixties drew them all
shooting up, fighting, pimping and whoring.
I Xeroxed it and papered my wall. We
would get baked and hysterical: Daisies

spread for Goofies, Donalds counted the bills,
Plutos lifted their legs in wet salutes.

"MASK" by ARTHUR GONZALEZ

AFTER THE PARTY

My friends visit, and I feast, storing up
memories, storing up memories for
when they're gone and I stand by the cupboard
with my hands, with my hands talking over
each other like they do when thoughts rupture

so fast over my head. If forever
were mine, I would be still as a painting
and reach the exquisite end of wonder.
Wonder why. Now my hands are recalling
their American faces. I suppose

we're the same around the world—but being
understood at last! Mother, I'll return.
Mother, I'll return, but first I'm knitting
this unforgettable, missing garment
from the way my friends are no longer here.

My hands knitting in the Sri Lankan sun,
knitting what's gone, knitting what's not yet gone.

SHIORI SHIMOMURA

IV

WHAT DIFFERENCE BETWEEN TREES AND BREAKERS?

—DEENA METZGER

DAVID FLEISCHMANN

A STORY

Once, a person quested to have an audience with The QueenKing
whose castles rise so glorious, megalithic, their amethyst
buttresses and sunglowing diamond towers stunned them to kneeling.
There in the Holy Royal Forest, ten-thousand furlongs distant,
our protagonists crawled closer to The Gates. Keeping to the path,

they found themselves journeying among many supplicant questors,
all of them living in their progress; thus surfacing a byway
in a multitudinous queue—encampments, markets, then restaurants—
petalling their forward motion, decelerating years from days,
brick houses from canvas tents, the wails of birth and mortal keening,

complex eddies and oddities of businesses and laws, ballets,
lottery tickets, parenting tips, videos, keypads, aglets
to Zambonis, astrophysics, zymurgy and all the ways we
forget that we forget what we once forgot...something we forget...
like the feeling of liking our smile as we smile it. Sit and rest

while time collapses and leaves the mind, while here our beloved pet,
for example, licks and licks our skin and what is unsettled sets.

!

"CHAIR" by KERRY VANDER MEER

A STORY

!

Gong splash, horn blast, trumpet fanfare, alarm bells—
at once mystery opens, memory calls

and all complex foldings and internal rhymes
vibrate in unison and fall to silence.
Here is the palace gate and the audience
we sought—our audience with The Essential—
it comes back! We remember this all at once,

and now we get to ask our One Big Question.
But first we must tell the backstory, the sense
of why we ask. Happily, there's no deadline.
It's our turn to unspool all that's woven us
all the way from that first "once upon a time."

It all started when a small sound sounded and
we wondered what it was. We wanted to find
out what mattered. We wanted to understand.
And we set out. We went to ask the divine
others who helped, pointed, urged, ushered us on…

"OAKLAND LOVE" by KERRY VANDER MEER

VISION QUEST VISION

Time starts to weave: a spider builds a web
over a small stream; it comes to hover;
a cone of wind washes an insect wave
toward us; contact hurries the spider;
we're aware how the tiny wing pairs stick.

Forest; spider; river; air; insects—here
comes the solid thing that pushes the swarm—
a woman—tan; hiking boots; long, black hair;
wearing a bikini; swinging Occam's
Razor—a broad stick to widen her way.

She could be a story in human form.
"Hey. Ya'll havin' a party over there?"
"It's a retreat." Her hips shift and she seems
to repeat a koan. "It's a party?"
I feel unsure. "It's a retreat." How her

weedy pubes spin out thick and uncontained.
Then she blazes on. The prior web's gone.

"FREEDOM" by HENRIK DRESCHER

Something out There

THE HALF OF IT

"It's human as a human eyeball,"
she says, "to fumble our deep knowledge
that the empty sky is teeming full
beyond our view, and the oceans—huge
and so crowded—go all the way down.

From the earliest age, we've drawn trees
as trunk, branches and leaves—never mind
the alleged subterranean
activities, the concealed details
we forget. That's natural—but we

don't remind ourselves that we forget.
One practice," she says, "is to wake up
to an intention of extending
ourselves into what we don't perceive,
letting our actions cross that blind edge

into those other realms. How will we
then modify what we do daily?"

"ROOTS" by JOE KOWALCZYK

QUERONS TO MORPHEUS (INFLECTION)

"Sing, my heart, the gardens you never walked."
—Rilke's Sonnets to Orpheus (Part II, 21)
translated by Joanna Macy and Anita Barrows

!

Glass
gardens!
Morpheus
dreamed of Bayon,
woke in Santa Cruz.

Figs ripen and ripen,
and each fruit listens—we swear
every iota, a silken
ear blooming, choosing—daring to hear
these praises and promises all at once!

Sing the gardens of Earth lush beyond compare!
How tallest blues and tiniest burrs may reveal
the moments in a lifetime of pain when the barrows
cradle your cells—and even in letting go you may see
those unreachable places—through moaning birth pains—reached again!

The clowns, saints, doctors, waters and figs you take within you deeply
weave your crumbling temples and ficuses into the great tapestry.

QUERONS TO MORPHEUS (REFLECTION)

This arm—hand—pencil—line grows visible—not a drawing of a thread,
but the thread itself—twisting albumen umbilicus letters

spinning, weaving, wearing the light—fruit—meat—tapestry faces.
As I'm the divine eye, I see stubbled cheeks, sweaty skin
in sweatpants swathed into earth grass sun air, with two legs
aimed uphill, ten toes up, ears grasstickled, pencil
in hand, on notebook, curling its winding said,

"i dont judge u," the *u* like this bald pate,
"including time all is forgiven."
  The cursive *all* loops a huge grace,
  melts into time. The gray flesh
  of words abides. Nascent

yawn in a forest.
Carapace sloughed.
Who rose wet?
Who tastes
sweet

  ?

138

QUERON

Within the everything everything is,
I felt pressed against a dividing skin,
a curtain that separates and marries
each something with its counterpart nothing.
On the reverse of the invisible,

the reasonable denizens of bardo
look so familiar, though they do strange things—
exact opposite parallel reasons
counterbalance both sides of anything.
The divide, Carroll's Caterpillar, says:

> *Who are you, unifying and zeroing,*
> *clay body pressed deep into a clay background?*
> *Do you invent names so that you needn't sing?*
> *Are you in the courtroom or on the playground—*
> *or around mushrooms just before revealing?*

> *The dimensionless alchemy between sound*
> *and silence underpins them both, I have found.*

DAVID FLEISCHMANN

PARADISE OUTDOORS

A canopy ravels from gray nacre,
the mountain's verdant newborn filigree.
As darkness and light flash, blessings accrue
unfurling in fern-tip complexities,
ushering the one space of the sacred.

Heaven is a gateless sanctuary
where my heart can run itself rabbit quick
sublimated in the nature of me,
andante rhythms of my walking stick,
gut and breath unbounded as an orchid.

Such hallowing glory demands a break:
that's when we go to church, temple or mall.
Under a roof only humans would make,
we collect into our scale and recall
the transports of sequoia and fungi.

But for prayer in the present, there's one hall:
the unroofed architecture of the all.

"LABYRINTH" by SHIORI SHIMOMURA

MEDITATION

The smooth stones blessed in Quan Yin's radius,
shaded by the rambling ficus, give way
to the pale paisleys of my bed sheets, mussed
in slow rising to the views of a day.
Soon the traffic of the busiest blocks

filters tidally through my maculae
and into my mouth, parted as I saw
on the serene Buddha faces arrayed
everywhere I went in Ayutthaya.
Where I sit like this is all one locus,

where my thoughts' weight and quantity withdraw
becoming as light and few as the skies
I've known. All seats are found in the same straw.
All breath is drawn from one well. As it slows
I count the cycles lifting away. Here

the meat of a being that sees and moves
recalls the unity it itself proves.

"LIGHT AND CRYSTAL" by KATINA HUSTON

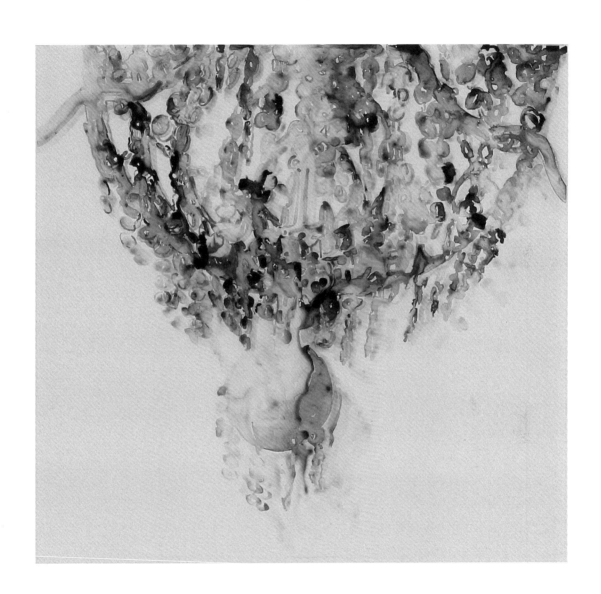

CONSIDER THE MACHINE

A) Assume the machine possesses
some minute fractional measure
of the soul of its creatrix.
B) Begin its automatic whirl.
C) Observe how all its procedures

execute in what seems a pure
ballet of physical science.
Mentionless variance accrues
and releases—the innocence
of physics plays on mechanics.

In its fraction of soul, a sense
of wobbling, a proto-tango,
quasi-Judo, or meta-dance,
physics pumping impish go-go
to some spiral of surrender.

D) Study the machine as it slows.
Its maker's friction makes it glow.

"THAT SHIT WAS DEEP" by WAYNE WHITE

I BELIEVE WHEN I RELENT

After Gabrielle Roth's 5Rhythms

I topple to rise up, then I tower to fall.
I've an upstart yen and an urge to surrender.
At whose bidding do I cross and re-cross the hall?
"I push backwards...I go forwards." —Larry Eigner.
"Nothing is true that isn't paradoxical."

—Kathy Altman. Her words add the waves to my gyre.
We are standing bubbles of wind, water and sand.
Since the floor is dancing, it's the perfect partner.
Head on the ground, feet researching the air firsthand,
what's down pushes up my fire, bruises my apple.

"In a field / I am the absence / of field." —Mark Strand.
Momentum tumbles my body, reads on my face.
My name flies off. You can call me "Blue Bandana."
Words and forms exchange gravity as we rephrase,
impelled by sounds, spirits, ourselves and each other,

and in peripatetic growth, we find a place.
Though prone to paroxysms, hail Us, full of grace.

CAROLE AMBAUEN

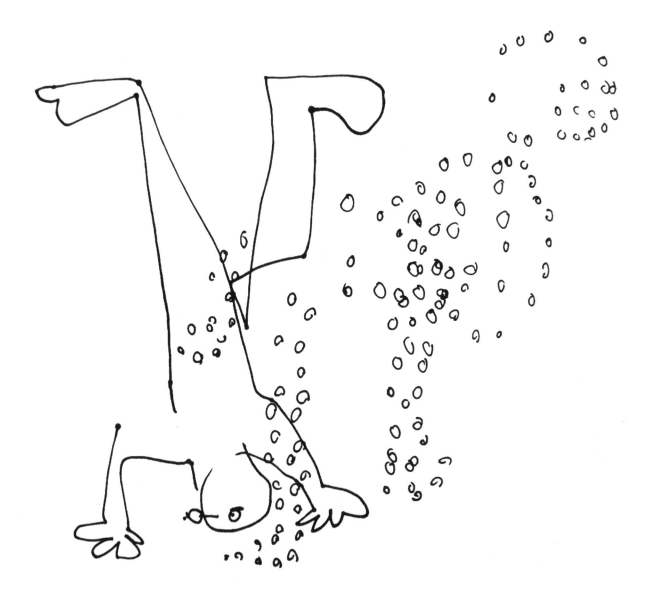

ALL ADDS UP

Now hear how musicians transcend maya
(or the illusions of self we each have).
Orchestras synthesize trembling mana,
and honey rises from the nascent hive.
Harmony is the honey of many.

To fuse in unison so as to live—
then to lose oneself—that's life's best honey.
Your strings ooze into the communal line
of woven sweet. Then the whole great world hones
its taste on this one music. It's zany

how the swarm of cells inside a bee's bones,
and the million details that make a home—
plus all your memories dumped from boxes—
don't make a mess. A clear lyric has come—
chaos looping and closing in a link,

that fits into a geometric comb
in a pure symphonic cellular womb.

""MATERIA #65" by DIANNE ROMAINE

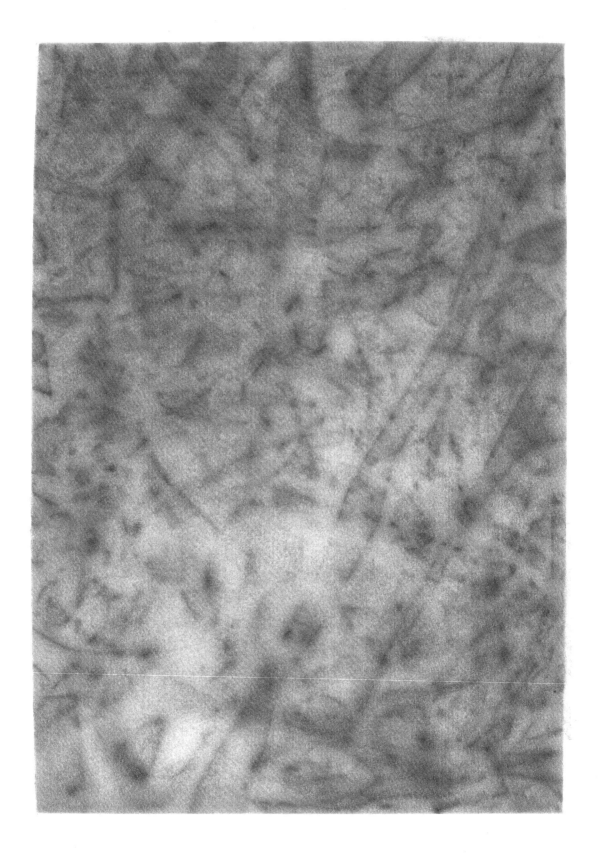

ALEPH

"This is a song about this." —*Gordon Gano*

One map
of sound
shows up,
around,
bebop!

Unbound
journeys,
new-found
holy
flute pipes,

hurdy-
gurdies,
dizzy
bird miles,
compound

over-
tones, words.

"PATH" by HENRIK DRESCHER

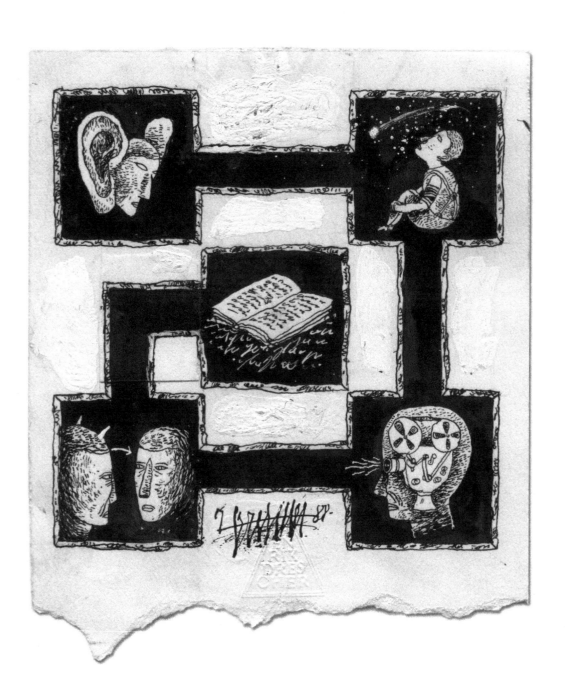

V

**NOT EVEN
THE SILENCE PURSUES ME.**

—PAUL AUSTER

MEETING THE DOCTOR

"Transplants are commonplace nowadays, even routine,
so no impediments remain to performing the process
on oneself. Pleased to meet you. Doctor Kenneth Frank—Ken's fine.
Transplants. *Symbiology.* You've probably guessed
the hand you shook just now was not always mine.

My gardener, a former cowpoke and prizefighter, possessed
musculature that was enviable, indeed.
When he quite unexpectedly passed,
I imagined a mutually beneficial arrangement. His cadaver agreed,
you might say. His arm lives on, serves me and retains

the strength and soul of his brawn and breed.
You felt him in the handshake. You met him, too,
just then. Sadly, his left hand would not accede
motor control (damned thing). But look here! Mismatched, it's true.
My left belonged to a concert harpist. Female, yes.

It was her dominant hand, so although in school,
I was right-handed, I now find myself ambidextrous—
and master of this limb's delicacy. My sutures
have become gestures with the power and finesse
of music. See my ankle? The fine needlework

scarcely left a scar. I'll never suffer again with as scabrous
an attachment as my first shoulder. I'm an artist now.
You'd almost think this was the leg I myself grew as a fetus.
Realize you are standing before a crowd,
all of us animated by a medical brain ahead of its future.

The procedure is costly, to be sure, but you learn to stop counting.
Take my card in case I might help you out, someday, somehow."

"THE DOCTOR" by CHRISTIAN ROMAN

ILL

Woke up a few inches above the sheets.
My bones were poking out of every pore.
The blankets hovered on my sharpest points.
I warned my waking wife, "Don't roll over.
I'm pokey again." "What? Ow. Okay. It's

going to be all right." She rose fast to pour
lotion into my hands. This I patted
on, leaving globs suspended from the hair-
thin needles covering me. She chattered
to make it all seem normal. "I think that's

a good reason to call in sick," she said.
"Would you do it?" I asked. "Okay. You go
to the garden. I'll call Guy." The sky bled
pinks and golds as I stopped and let my toes'
tender skin greet the cold, bare soil. My core

felt warm though frost stood in the garden rows,
and I was naked as a winter rose.

QUERON 18

Shall I compare thee to a winter's day?
Thou art more still and far more temperate.
Rough winds do shake the manor's windowpanes,
and winter's lease hath all too short a date.
But thy eternal winter shall not fade

so long as in the virgin's blood you bathe,
nor lose possession of that fair thou owest;
nor shall Death brag thou wanderest in his shade
when in eternal crimson-thirst thy ghost
administers its soul-suck to thy prey.

Yet in aerial din cold Death may boast
his servant to the Netherworlds beguiles.
Innocent, I laid near thee, Twilit Host,
but, O, thy soul within a nadir lie.
By dawn we both drank deep the salt of Fate.

So long as men can breathe, or eyes can cry,
so long we shun the light, we canst not die.

MARK HAMMERMEISTER

Hammermeister

THE PALE MAN

I am a chef. I have seen nearly three
centuries because I have learned to cook
cuisine of formidable sorcery.
My orchard yields only weeds. You can look.
I fetch a pailful to the scullery,

warp creeping jenny, pokeweed and hemlock
into aromatic strawberry crepes.
It takes weeks of precise hand-and-eye work,
metamorphosing moss to muscat grapes—
and all the while I am madly hungry.

Springtime to springtime. That's the time it takes
to set the banquet, serve the trap, then rest
my eyes, side by side, on the pewter plate.
There's nothing then but to wait, unconscious,
until, at last, some door admits a crook.

More than anything, I love having guests.
I count the skulls, the times I've been so blessed.

"ALL-SEEING HAND" by ERIC LINDSEY

ZOMBIE MOVIE CLIMAX

This is a zombie movie scenario starring me
as me myself, and also as the zombie who shambles
patiently through the abandoned midnight neighborhood scene:
Hero-me stops running, grabs zombie-me by the lapels.
"Wake up, damn it! Smell the roses in the mausoleum!"

Close up on two faces. The living one: "Look at yourself!"
A spark ignites in the zombie's eyes. "You're animated!"
The room spirals and goes bright in a frenzy of cellos.
Their clutch breaks. The hero cries, "You don't have to be so dead!"
The zombie's mouth closes, then opens and moans, "Oh. I see.

Animation. It's all. I have. So. It has. To be. Good.
Enough. For me." Dawn's first rosy finger touches the east.
Zomb-me turns to look. On the face of it, life doesn't hold
much for the vitally challenged. On the other wasted
hand, might a cadaver carry on, exploring the hills,

riding a cargo ship to Chile, learning how to dance,
dining with—who knows who—or what—*on tacos de sesos?*

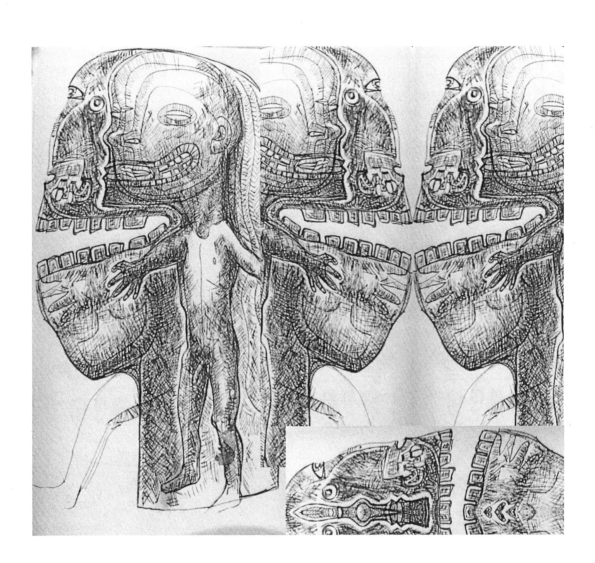

WARTS AND ALL

At the marketplace, my eggs sell themselves.
My basil's gone by nine, and my rhubarb
pies fetch a creamy price, so my walk back's
weightless. It's just me and my empty cart.
You see? It doesn't matter that my face

scares bats. By day, my visage stays downward
on dirt, scales and coins; but my nose lifts up
ambling back with a jingle as the stars
glint like tavern lamplights off raised ale cups.
If I can jingle, who could say I'm cursed?

I was foul and fourteen when my pop-pop
pulled me bodily out to the garden,
bent my stubborn knees beside the turnips,
gave me a trowel, looked in me and said: "Start.
Warts and all. Start." My body sprouted warm,

like the soil converting itself to food.
That day I became apprentice to dirt.

ANGELIN MILLER

UNEARTHLY WHIZ

Sparked by Wretches and Jabberers

A's for appearance, the first shapes one sees,
and mine don't help to make my beauty's case.
Beard bramble, beach-ball belly, buzzard eyes,
bottom bite—and bejesus, my face—these
cleave all my encounters to choppy seas.

Do you think you'd do with a self like this:
a knack for remunerative visions
but no rein on the way you come across?
My gifts for profit get badly shaken
by swiveled necks, bulged eyes and guts that seize.

Fed up with shrugging off being passed on,
I started to keep my trumpet muted.
I've mucked through anger and introversion—
but it couldn't last. If you're like me, friend,
you've your fair share of shareable genius.

So we aim to express it before zed:
what we've got here is the premium blend.

"DAILY MONSTER PAPERS 214" by STEFAN G. BUCHER

THE ULTIMATE DINGO KING OF THE SUPERHERO BALLET

"I am not the chosen one. I am the only one." —*James Hellwig*

In the oil of spectacle
you burned as the purest wick
pitching Caliban tantrums,
flying from the turnbuckle,
lifting the coliseum—

and every time you spoke, blood
stars in the noonday sky rained
lawnmowers, snakes and earthquakes
nosediving the gods' storm rage
on YOU! I have heard the call

of your deadly masquerade,
cheered your unfaltering war
even when your balance failed.
You were an ass, I heard, but
that was just the man whose back

you rode, whose veins pumped your fire
who, at last, gave you his heart.

"FUNNEL VISION" by HENRIK DRESCHER

ECLIPSE DURING SATURN RETURN

O:
A black hole
in a ruddy glow.
The moon went incognito.
The earth followed suit. We reeled below

like drunken twentysomething werewolves in snow.
Two men gone bloody under the penumbra. When clans
of carnivores meet their brethren, we howl concertos—
hunt and howl long Os in transcendent, blood-bound harmonies.
Sleek-furred, open-nostrilled, taut-muscled, Josho and I

twined our vulpine, astronomical supplications
for connective joy—for mirrors, partners, orbits—
we caterwauled our throats raw for women.
When the frozen white light returned,
we panted our prayers, so

blessed by earth-moon
union.

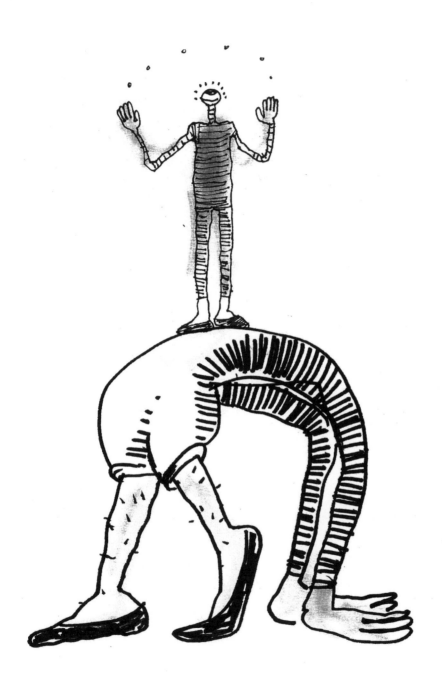

HEATHER WILCOXON

VI

**IN NORTH AMERICA TIME STUMBLES ON
WITHOUT MOVING**

—ADRIENNE RICH

WHEN YOU'RE LIVING IN A VAN DOWN BY THE RIVER

for David

Future generations, Chris Farley
was a corpulent comedian
a little like John Belushi—if
you know him. Both men played their poundage.
Chris did a Chippendale's parody.

(That's a male stripper.) He was undone
young by his weight, and drugs. In Vegas,
where cosplayers busk for tips downtown,
a fat man had Farley's hair, glasses,
manners and stripper dance to a T.

My brother was transported by his
embodiment. I took their picture
and a movie as they did the shticks.
David gave him a buck, then two more.
An artist, too, he lives cannily

and values showing gratitude for
homages with such funny sorrow.

"FARLEY" by MARK BELL

THE INCHES BETWEEN

When we joked as kids about improbable fates,
we chose meteor strikes. This was before the Web.
Our sense of distance suited analog date stamps.
We clicked our tongues each day for the hostages kept.
Four hundred. Americans had someone to hate.

This morning, maybe the jogger's curvy rear end
shook the workaday rhythm of the crossing guard,
and timing failed. I jumped on the brake. Momentum
flew my briefcase to the floor—but another car
arrowed through, interlocking like a gear's tooth straight

into the gap between clockwork tick and murder.
And today in Iraq, Nigeria, Boston,
and yesterday in Somalia, Syria…
Meteors really did fall on Russia. Newtown…
This morning, my mind's jumpy as the Internet—

I wish I'd have stopped, but the jogger just ran on
with only a glance toward the imminent headline.

WELCOMING THE NEW NORMAL

late September, 2008

Who left the money for the breeze
to squander? Grant returns to pulp
in the gutter. The rosemary
bush wears Benjamin like a cap.
"It's an ill wind," neighbors decree,

but the sun still lights up our crap,
all the doodads we've said thanks for
now tagged and arranged on our tarps.
But no one's selling wrapped food or
wool blankets, so nobody trades

in currency—only rumors.
At least we have fresh rosemary
to make our spaghetti gourmet.
Gift-giving traditions may be
impeached this year—but you don't shop

for what I want most. Luckily
my favorite gift from you is free.

TOM FRANCO

NO ONE MOVES

Public chess set in the Galleria
with 4-foot kings and queens: I've never seen
anybody play. You'd have to be a
chess player to suggest putting one in.
Maybe some assistant set it via

the mall manager. I know that a queen
can be pushed by a pawn—but nobody
plays as far as I've seen. I eat frozen
yogurt, listening to podcasts at three.
Watching a match would seem hilarious

in San Francisco's stylishly stifled
downtown daylight. I imagine someone
putting lipstick on the kings or heaping
the pieces in a bacchanal pattern
after hours. They may in the Mission,

but here the gates get drawn down and fastened.
Thirty-two pieces stand unmolested.

ROZ CHAST

THE LIBRARY

for Marna Scooter Cascadia and John Fox

John and I ordered two slices
and a raspberry soda each.
We ate and took turns reciting
snips and strophes within easy reach,
chuckling, focusing or sighing

to fit the words, until our speech
joined together at Innisfree.
We chanted that secluded beach
into being. John beamishly
coaxed in Yeats' cat, Minnaloushe,

who puzzled the moon, far and wee—
and so we came upon Cummings
hiccupping that typography
over our paper plates and crumbs.
We stood up. It was time to teach

of what had passed and what would come,
how poems make a honeycomb.

SNIPS & STROPHES

who puzzled the moon, far & wee

how
poems
make a
honeycomb

YEATS' ISLAND

May I go where you go, William,
that island where you live alone?
In truth, I do. I've seen your farm
early in bean-planting season.
Like you, I take no boat, nor swim.

No soul is there except the sound.
I act as an intern butler
when I visit, cleaning your panes
of air, emptying the kettle
of linnets' wings. I love your room.

I've been trying to tune some wattles
into a sort of wind chime when
an email comes with a subtle
ping, and I'm suddenly returned
to this gray desk—and somewhat stunned

to find my assigned space unchanged.
One more second—I'll dive back in.

"YEATS' ISLAND" by JOE KOWALCZYK

FLAT PAGE IN A BOOK OF FACES

Today's news: Pick a Card.
What's Burning and Whose Face.
The graphic. The music.
Supreme Court Bungles Case.
Click the top story first—

but first the latest choice—
and first the finger falls—
the digital bouncer
administers the hall.
Cute kitten tricks bulldog.

Some actor with the balls
to act like the czar (he
is) pissed on the fourth wall.
Ex-Fans Burn DVDs.
It's the Day of the Dead

for Auks, Experts Agree.
Mines Leaking Quicksilver;
Domestic Refugees.
Geeks Defends Czar's Movies.
Subtitle. Sidebar. Scroll:

the shoes you browsed last week.
The actor wrote a book
and it's smoking, set fire.
He was crude to his cook.
Strange behavior in bees.

Click and scroll. But first, Like
the picture your niece took.

EATING FREEDOM

Your most basic process
that you may still control
when all other choices
get taken from you—pulled
off like skin or voice—is

picking up the morsel,
putting it in your mouth.
Chew and chew and swallow.
You are hungry. Outside
of that fact, your actions

are yours. Maybe. Without
that freedom, what are you?
A can with two snout holes
gasping for some human
prayer in the captor's will.

We trust our food to feed,
but YouTube "Yasiin Bey."

From Guantánamo to Berkeley

In October 2011 the Berkeley City Council passed a Resolution to close Guantanamo Prison and welcome cleared-for-release detainees to settle in Berkeley. This makes Berkeley the first city in the U.S. to welcome detainees. Djamel Ameziane is a famous Algerian-born European-trained chef who the U.S. cleared for release in 2008, but he's still stuck in Guantanamo.

To find out more about Djamel Ameziane's current status and to donate to his resettlement fund please contact:

Berkeley No More Guantanamos
info@nogitmos.org (510) 333-6097
www.closegitmo.org

REASONABLE DOUBT V. ABIDING CONVICTION

The judge, if he were I, would smoke a doob
every night at six. He'd return from court,
leave his lightless clothes bunched on the bamboo
floor then go naked into the kitchen
to fix himself a vodka and Yoohoo.

He'd take it all with him to the hot tub
to lose definitions to the bubbles.
The niggling asides from the Princeton brat
prosecutor; defense counsel's large boobs;
jurors moping in and out of the room—

and that girl at life's buffet of trouble,
the sift of blood marks from alleged violence,
the unseeing windows of those suburbs
where something boiled her grief into grievance
that cooled quick, like skin on gravy recants

its heat. Mistrial. Lost to the night's silence,
his honor's thoughts are not in evidence.

"HOT TUB" by MARK BELL

I SUFFERED SOMEWHAT.

—title from Ferlighetti, impetus from Pineda

They say my name, but I didn't give it.
They got into me before I knew it.
I wince whenever someone says, "Who's they?"
We all know they. We trusted them to do
the science. (Now, I would like to unsay

my vote and shut the lights if it's not too
matterless to sway one vague nucleus.
Or I could join the chorus of renewed
believers who recommitted because
breath still follows breath, night still follows day—

and where there's no choice, it feels like a choice.)
They're the ones who told those people to hire
the folks who contracted those who would foist
the blame on those who killed the engineers
paid by the leaders elected by they——

They who broke off a piece of solar fire,
who wrack it and bring the blood to my door.

HEATHER WILCOXON

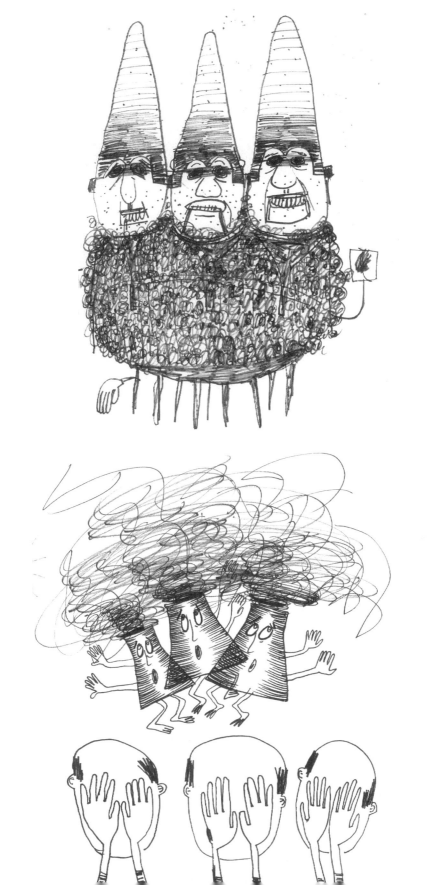

POST-APOCALYPSE FOR DUMMIES

Food and water. Guard these with guns,
and if you can, keep them loaded.
There's Reese's Peanut Butter Cups
stockpiled by two boys, ten years old—
open your mouth and walk right up.

Some kids might not shoot if beseeched
by an old man with six orphans.
Make your fort far above the ground.
You'll need a swing set to get in.
Postcard blockhouses in the sun

wait nervously while mobs of men
rock and topple the clock tower.
Sip water and watch. The children
are quiet with their vantage view.
People are living on the bridge.

When honeybees became too few,
there's nothing Superman could do.

OLD WORLD WORSHIP

"Is this the baseline, living, living at last, without all of civilization's tortured overlay?"
—Cecile Pineda

The idiom *down with something*
means bring it literally or
symbolically closer to earth.
That means: *exalt it with honor.*
Revere it beside or within

the precious ground that we are born
to be on. So: down with our dreams.
Down with the cornucopias
that grace the tables in our homes.
Down with our lives. Down with our deaths.

Up with the zeal that cuts atoms!
Up with spur-and-bridle fever!
Down with resting uranium!
Ionosphere take the monsters
of bodiless information!

Holy is the altar herself,
this flesh of Gaia—down with Her!

TWIN PEAKS WITH STEVE

He marches ahead of me
forward through the foggy veil.
Now and then, he turns to see
that I follow on the trail.
I put faith in his body.

He is generous to smile
when the ground gets steep and slick,
and the steps become a trial.
I can hear our bone joints click
until the path goes even.

We come panting in the thick
air to a peak with no view—
not to find out why we're sick
nor to ask what we should do.
Amazingly the candle

he lights keeps flame as the dew
settles in us through and through.

LAUREN ARI

WHAT EXPERIENCES

With Janice Sandeen

Curtains

drawn

reveal open
windows   beyond dawn:
consider our selves finely woven

iotas in the waft between unfixed and foregone.

We are as lines among tesseract foldings. Each of us is a wall—

one sticky, critical wall—built to function within honeycombing complexities,
convexities of inside-outside decision forks—spun, spanning, spinning and spawned—

*"…experience awaits and awaits, yet also passes by us, pondering us like the creatures
we are. Experience having us, we are possessed by that which dawns on us, possessed
in measure, great and small."*

Experience hears us wearing it, wears us as we have it—here—where a line drawn is
drawn like an inhalation;

and we might feel impelled like bees or fan-handed barnacles

to wave constantly in the ocean's intimate infinity—
visions, revises, calls and recalls

you and me,
hanging upon

any

sea.

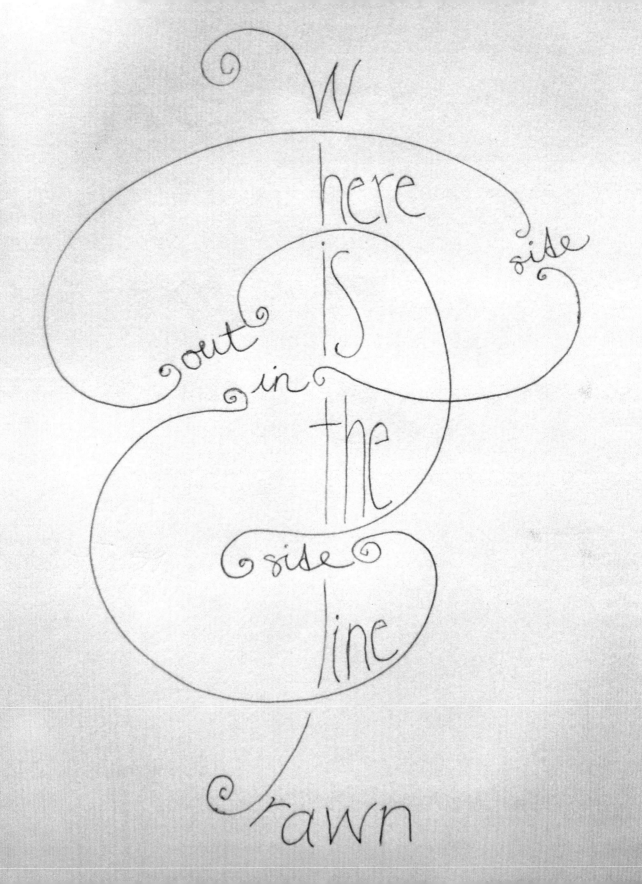

THE ARTISTS

Chuck H. Alston (page 33) was born and raised in the San Francisco Bay Area and studied art at the Ruth Asawa School of the Arts. He was awarded a young artist's Certificate of Honor from the San Francisco board of supervisors. Watch his art career take off at charleshalston.wix.com/official.

Carole Ambauen (page 149) grew up in Switzerland hiking the Alps. She trained as a graphic designer and moved to Portland in 2001, where she had spent time as an exchange student. Today she lives in California's Bay Area and works as a graphic designer and a licensed craniosacral therapist. Online: caroleambauen.com.

Sybil Archibald (page 59) was born in Los Angeles in 1968. As a teenager she became obsessed with the process of birth. Later she realized her obsession was with the nature of creativity itself. In college, she was diagnosed with scleroderma, a rare autoimmune disease. As her illness kept her from fully pursuing art, it forced her deep inside, ultimately showing her the face of the Divine. As her acceptance of her illness has grown, so has her connection to her artistic process. See sybilarchibald.com.

Lauren Ari (pages 21, 65, 93, 98, 125, 155, 202) is a teacher and studio artist with work in collections internationally including the permanent collection of The de Young Museum in San Francisco. Visit laurenari.com.

Mirabai Rose Ari (pages 48, 63) is a student at Madera Elementary School. Born in Berkeley in 2006, she currently pursues art, acting, storytelling, music and dance.

Carol Aust (page 43) works in acrylic on canvas and wood panels at her studio in Oakland, California. Her figurative paintings are emotionally charged narrative fragments infused with mysterious tension and secrecy. Her paintings express a wide range of human experience, and she often places figures in precarious environments where anything could happen. Carol's art is represented in private collections throughout the United States. Enjoy more at carolaust.com.

Mark Bell (pages 177, 193) is an "Undeclared Major" creative, working in photography, illustration, digital design and light fixture fabrication. If you remember Yahoo's animated illustration on their landing pages, he was that guy. Now he pursues his love of design by making home lighting out of repurposed toys, camping toasters, fire-hose nozzles, skateboards, and just about anything. When he's not restoring his vintage cars, or trying to get his teenage kids to hang out with him, he's usually at his Berkeley shop, Omega Lighting & Design. Swing by and say hello.

Stefan G. Bucher (page 169) is the man behind 344lovesyou.com and the popular online drawing and story-telling experiment, dailymonster.com. His books include *100 Days of Monsters* and *344 Questions: The Creative Person's Do-It-Yourself Guide to Insight, Survival, and Artistic Fulfillment*. Check out his Monster Maker app at tinyurl.com/monstermaker

Marna Scooter Cascadia (page 185) thrives in the Pacific Cascadia bioregion amidst dragon-shaped permaculture gardens while pursuing work at the intersection of ecological restoration and earth wisdom. She cultivates poetry as healing and enjoys nurturing and synergizing creative collaborations. Her friendship with Daniel Ari began thirty years ago under the breeze-blown trees at UC Irvine. Scooter has appeared in journals such as *MiPoesias*, *We'Moon*, and *Pearl*, and several anthologies. See her work at The Institute for Earth Regenerative Studies (earthregenerative.org) and Moonifest (moonifest.org), a creative arts nonprofit.

Jeannine Chappell (page 83) was born in Atlanta, Georgia. She began painting in her twenties, and worked in mixed media on paper for years, exhibiting around the Bay Area. In the mid-nineties she combined her love for working on paper with computer art to produce works inspired by nature. She has produced several books; among the most recent is *This Has Happened* with poet David Brehmer about the tragic death of her son in a car crash. Visit jeanninechappell.com.

Roz Chast (page 183) grew up in Brooklyn, New York and attended the Rhode Island School of Design. She began contributing to *The New Yorker* in 1978 and became a staff cartoonist in 1979. Since then, she has contributed over 1,000 cartoons and ten covers to the magazine. She has also illustrated several children's books, most notably with the humor writer Patricia Marx and the actor Steve Martin. Her most recent cartoon collection is *Theories of Everything: Selected, Collected, and Health-Inspected Cartoons of Roz Chast*. In 2014, Bloomsbury published an illustrated memoir about the last years of her parents' lives. More at rozchast.com.

R. Crumb (pages 41, 47, 69, 87, 139) emerged as a preeminent sequential artist in the 1960s with *Zap Comix*, the first successful example of "underground comix." His satirical, counter-culture characters such as Fritz the Cat, Mr. Natural and Angelfood McSpade took their place in popular culture along with his cartoon slogan "Keep on Truckin'." His later work became more autobiographical, exploring his sex obsessions and his adult life with artist Aline Kominsky-Crumb. In 1994, he was the subject of the documentary, *Crumb*, directed by Terry Zwigoff. Currently living in the south of France, Crumb came out with *The Illustrated Book of Genesis* in 2009, a 200-page book that took four years to complete. His official site: crumbproducts.com

Veronica De Jesus (page 81) was born in 1970. She is Chinese, Puerto Rican and Italian. She earned her BFA from the San Francisco Art Institute in 1998 and her MFA from UC Berkeley in 2003. She currently lives, makes art and teaches in Los Angeles. Check out veronicadejesus.com.

Henrik Drescher (pages 105, 133, 153, 171) is a Danish artist whose illustrative work grows out of his notebooks, journals and paintings. His editorial illustrations frequently appear in *The New York Times, The Washington Post, Newsweek, Time* and *Rolling Stone*; and he has written and illustrated several books for children and adults including *Pat the Beastie, Simon's Book,* and *McFig & McFly.* More at hdrescher.com.

Joakim Drescher (page 23) mainly draws and produces limited-edition artwork, but also dabbles in audio recording and songwriting. Born in Copenhagen, Denmark. Joakim has lived all over the world and currently resides in California's Bay Area. Check out jdrescher.tumblr.com.

Gitty Duncan (page 85, 99, 175) is a Berkeley-based artist, fashion designer, puppeteer and teacher. Transplanted from New York, she studied ceramic sculpture and glassblowing at the Rhode Island School of Design, then earned her MFA from UC Davis. Gitty co-created Puppets and Pie, an after-school program and summer camp for kids.

Lauren Elder (pages 15, 16) is an artist, arts educator and activist who came of age in the late 1960's during the beginnings of the movements for social and environmental justice. Those ideals continue to inform her practice. Her early body of work focused on environmentally situated performances. Recently she has shifted towards creating permanent environments to frame the dramas and comedies of everyday life. Projects are supported by public funds, local businesses and the "sweat equity" of participants. She was trained in Sculpture at UCLA and Landscape Architecture at UC Berkeley. Visit laurenelder.com to learn more.

Reza Farazmand (page 19) is a cartoonist who lives in Los Angeles. He makes a webcomic called Poorly Drawn Lines and enjoys using the Internet. Get some laughs at poorlydrawnlines.com.

David Fleischmann (pages 17, 31, 127, 141) is a caricature artist living in Laguna Beach, California. Hire him for your next party or event, and he will draw hilarious, flattering cartoon portraits of your guests. David also creates fine art, including painted palm frond masks and abstract "vision paintings" of images that appear to him on the edge of dreaming. See his art at freeradicalsings.blogspot.com.

Michael Fleischmann (page 109) studied journalism, art and design at the University of Missouri in Columbia. His first job was directing and designing animations in a PR department. Seeking more creative work, he moved to New York to work in motion graphics. His animation experience led to a job at NBC where he remains today, making on-air graphics and animations for The Today Show. In his spare time he takes photographs, processes some into 3D images, and shares them with other hobbyists.

John Yoyogi Fortes (page 197) studied painting at California State University, Fresno. His paintings have been exhibited worldwide and are held in numerous collections including the Asian American Art Centre in New York, the Nevada Museum of Art in Reno, the Triton Museum of Art, and the Crocker Art Museum in California. He has received numerous grants and awards including the Commissioners Artist Fellowship from the Sacramento Metropolitan Arts Commission, a Visual Artist Fellowship from the California Arts Council, and a grant from the Joan Mitchell Foundation in New York. John currently resides in Sacramento. More at johnyoyogifortes.com.

Tom Franco (page 181) was born in Palo Alto, California, the second of three boys. He studied art at UC Santa Cruz and California College of the Arts. In 1996, Tom made meditation a daily practice and part of his art making process. Through dance ensemble work and Tai Chi, Tom found his direction for doing visual arts in groups instead of alone. Performance became a central element in his understanding of visual representation. In 2005 Tom co-created the Firehouse Art Collective in Berkeley. It is a space for artists of all disciplines to make community and culture, and for art patrons and collectors to buy cutting edge art of lasting value. Today The Firehouse Art Collective has five Northern California locations. Learn more at firehouseartcollective.blogspot.com.

Sheila Ghidini (page 97) was born in Connecticut. She attended University of Hartford Art School and did graduate work at Cranbrook Academy of Art. She completed an MFA in sculpture at UC Berkeley, receiving the Sylvan and Pam Coleman Memorial Fellowship. Sheila was an artist-in residence at The Headlands Center for the Arts and The American Academy in Rome. She has received grants from the Wallace Alexander Gerbode Foundation, the Krasner-Pollack Foundation, the San Francisco Arts Commission, the Marcelle Labaudt Memorial Fund, Rockefeller Foundation and the Connecticut Commission on the Arts. Sheila is represented by Chandra Cerrito Contemporary in Oakland, CA. More at sheilaghidiniprojectspace.com.

Regina Gilligan (page 189) begins her work with memories that puzzle through her experiences and stretch back to her earliest asking, "But why, mommy?" She likes researching disasters, ancient cultures, poetic discourses on the world's pressing problems, noble persons, false premises, nature and natural inclinations. Regina explores ideas through any materials that may convey the story, weaving recycled paper, metal, cloth, paint, etc. into a collective investigation of materials, processes, and concepts.

Andrew Goldfarb (page 121), AKA The Slow Poisoner, is a one-man surrealistic rock band from San Francisco. His sound is rootsy and weird, something akin to a hoedown on Mars. His latest album is the rock opera, *Lost Hills*. Andrew is also an illustrator and author. He draws a comic strip called *Ogner Stump's One Thousand Sorrows* and paints velvet portraits of cryptic mystics and sad hobo clowns. His novels *Hypno-Hog's Moonshine Monster Jamboree* and *Slub Glub in the Weird World of the Weeping Willows* have been published by Eraserhead Press. Dive into his world at theslowpoisoner.com.

Arthur Gonzalez (page 123) has been creating and exhibiting work for over 30 years. Primarily a ceramic sculptor, Gonzalez's art is included in collections worldwide. In 2007, he published *The Art of Rejection*, a book of drawings done on the rejection letters he had amassed over the years. Teaching art since the '80s, he is currently a tenured professor at the California College of Arts in Oakland. Art at arthurgonzalez.com.

Roberta Gregory (page 67) has created comics since the 1970s, appearing in "undergrounds" like *Wimmen's Comix* and her own title, *Dynamite Damsels*. In the 90s she produced her Fantagraphics solo title, *Naughty Bits;* and her Bitchy Bitch character has been translated into several languages and appeared in a weekly strip, live theater productions and an animated television series. Roberta also created the *Winging It* graphic novel, *Sheila and the Unicorn*, and *Artistic Licentiousness.* She is currently working on a Bitchy graphic novel, the Mother Mountain series, and more. She recently published *True Cat Toons* and *Follow Your Art*, a book of travel comics. To keep up with her, friend her on Facebook or visit robertagregory.com and truecattoons.com.

Bill Griffith (page 79) is a prolific American cartoonist best known for his daily comic strip *Zippy The Pinhead*, which is the credited source of the catchphrase "Are we having fun yet?" See zippythepinhead.com for more.

Mark Hammermeister (page 161) is a digital painter and illustrator from the Detroit area. He grew up on *Mad Magazine*, monster movies and sci-fi. He has done work for advertising, packaging and editorial and has shown in many galleries. His clients include *Playboy*, LucasFilm, Paramount Pictures, Hanna-Barbera Animation Studios, Citibank, and *The New York Observer*. See more at markdraws.com.

Elizabeth Hird (page 39) has an MFA from the San Francisco Art Institute and has been teaching art to children, teens, and adults since 1986. She exhibits her work professionally, and her art appears in many private and public collections. For the last four winters, she has traveled all over the world practicing traditional art forms, dancing, and filming dance and nature. Elizabeth leads Paint Dancing, a practice that explores the intersection of dance and visual art through whole-body movement. See her art online at elizabethhird.com.

Katina Huston (page 145) was born in San Francisco in 1961. She trained in the History of Fine Art at New York University with an amazing group of scholars—Janson, Rosenblum, Varnedoe, Edward Sullivan—while learning several computer languages, now obsolete. Her art has been the subject of ten solo shows in the last half dozen years including shows in Japan, Sweden and Italy. Her drawings are in the collections of the San Francisco Fine Art Museum, Yale University Art Gallery, and Steve Wynn's collection at Wynn Casino Las Vegas. Ms. Huston currently lives and works in Alameda, California and around the world. katinahuston.com.

Kato Jaworski (page 45) painted daily experience, recording visual moments using simple materials including recycled elements. Kato lived and worked in Richmond, California, supporting her creative life and the creative life of her community as the education director at the Richmond Art Center. She died at home in early 2015.

Matt Jones (page 71) was born in Wales and has worked in the animation industry for twenty years. He has worked as a storyboard artist on animated features for Warner Bros. Sony, Aardman, Europacorp and Pixar. He is now based in Los Angeles. See mattjonezanimation.blogspot.com.

Chamisa Kellogg (page 173) has been drawing since her hand was barely big enough to hold a pen. She works mostly in watercolor, inks and pencil. While her primary interest is story illustration, she occasionally dives into the wild world of fine art. Chamisa lives and works in Portland, and has a degree in illustration from the Rhode Island School of Design. Visit chamisakellogg.com.

Joe Kowalczyk (pages 135, 187) is an award-winning sculptor, painter and draftsman who has been contributing to the arts community in the Bay Area since receiving his BFA in ceramics from California College of the Arts in 2006. Along with making studio work, Joe is a ceramic instructor at Creative Growth Art Center. He runs a kiln repair business (kilnspecialist.com) and is co-founder/co-director of FM, a fine arts gallery and community of artist studios in the Oakland Art Murmur district (FMoakland.com). More at joko.us.

Ines Kramer (page 61) traveled between the U.S. and Latin America before living in New York and ultimately the Bay Area. Her art is a synthesis of each region's visual cues—tropical greens, coastal grays, southwestern earth tones. After studying painting in New York City's Parsons and Art Students League and San Francisco State University, she began exhibiting, gaining national exposure by 1993. Kramer's work is in public and private collections. She was recently awarded a commission to create a suite of paintings for Alameda County's Highland Hospital, and she was featured in Nancy Reyner's book, *Acrylic Innovation*. Visit ineskramer.com.

Krystine Kryttre (page 111) was appointed to the Bureau of Underground Cartoonists in 1985. Her comics have appeared in *Viper, Cannibal Romance, Raw, Weirdo, Snake Eyes, Twisted Sisters, Artforum,* and others. She produced two solo books, *Death Warmed Over,* and *The #@@*! Coloring Book.* Her paintings and taxidermy sculptures have been showcased in three solo shows at La Luz De Jesus Gallery in Los Angeles and in various group shows hither and thither. She lives in Los Angeles. Meet her at kryttre.com.

Eric Lindsey (cover, page 163) is a North American artist residing in San Francisco, California—the city of his birth. He is an art director by trade, a musician, and the father of two young men. He began his creative career within a cloak of anonymity in search of infamy through graffiti. He has since transformed his creative endeavors into a career in art and design.

Liz Maxwell (page 137) earned her BS at UC Berkeley, then studied art in summer sessions and weekend classes at the California College of Arts. She has now been painting for 35 years, and has been a (nearly) fulltime artist since retiring from two previous careers. Her work has been shown in exhibitions nationwide. She is represented by Hang Gallery and SFMOMA Artists Gallery in San Francisco. Her work is motivated by interests in nature, mathematics, cosmology and the wonders of outer space. See more of her work at lizmaxwell.com.

Angelin Miller (pages 77, 91, 167) represents the natural world through painting, drawing and textiles. Connect at angelinmiller.com.

Tony Millionaire (page 29) writes and draws the adventures of Sock Monkey, published by Dark Horse Comics since 1998. He also created the syndicated comic strip, *Maakies,* collected by Fantagraphics, who also published his graphic novels, *Billy Hazelnuts* and *Billy Hazelnuts and the Crazy Bird.* He has won five Eisner Awards, three Harvey Awards, and an Ignatz Award. *Maakies* was adapted to the small screen in 1998 for *Saturday Night Live* and in 2008 as *The Drinky Crow Show* for Cartoon Network's Adult Swim. His art has appeared in *The Believer, The New Yorker* and *The Wall Street Journal,* and on record covers including They Might Be Giants' *Then; The Earlier Years,* Jon Spencer's *Heavy Trash,* and Elvis Costello's *Secret, Profane and Sugarcane* and *National Ransom.* He lives in Pasadena, CA with his family. Check out maakies.com.

Doug Minkler (page 191) is a San Francisco Bay Area printmaker specializing in fund raising, outreach and educational posters. Past collaborations include work with ILWU, Rain Forest Action Network, The SF Mime Troupe, ACLU, The Lawyers Guild, CISPES, United Auto Workers, Africa Information Network, Ecumenical Peace Union, ADAPT, Cop Watch, Street Sheet and Veterans for Peace. You can purchase original hand made screen prints at dminkler.com.

Art Moura (pages 154, 165) studied Electronic Engineering at San Jose State University and Art History in San Francisco. He spent a year in Madrid making art and studying Picasso's *Guernica*. His drawings were published in *Ripper*, a Punkzine, which led to his first exhibition and gave him a thirst for showing work. Moura moved to Sebastopol, California in 2000 where he continues to create and exhibit work, hold art parties and manifest a Life in Art. See his work at artmouraarts.com.

Jay Musler (page 25) is a glass artist with work in collections worldwide. He has created and shown work for more than 30 years.

Allan Peterson (page 179) is a visual artist and poet living in Gulf Breeze, Florida and Ashland, Oregon. You can see more of what he does at allanpeterson.net.

Aisha Rahim (page 103) was born Ruth Ward in Mobile, Alabama in 1940. She moved to Oakland, California as a young girl and began making art. Her mother died when Aisha was nine. In her twenties she had a daughter and a son. In her forties, Aisha was diagnosed with lupus, and she spent her last decade in a wheel chair. Her artwork in this book comes from 1992, the last year of her life. It was provided by her daughter, Soyinka Rahim, who is a performer, teacher and spiritual leader. BIBO.

Shraya L. Rajbhandary (pages 75, 95) was born in Nepal and started drawing as early as he can remember, even getting in trouble for doodling in class. He came to the U.S. to study art at Park University in Kansas City, MO, and graduated with degrees in Graphic Design and Fine Arts. He currently lives and makes art in California. See what he does at shraya-rajbhandary.com.

Dianne Romaine (page 151), a fifth generation San Franciscan, graduated from San Francisco Art Institute in 1988. She has taught art at San Francisco City College since 1990, and her work has been exhibited nationwide. Her art making comes from noticing the subtle patterns in life, and in questioning what is and isn't essential. Seeking elemental solutions, she has reduced her palette to very simple forms and an economy of materials. The results are contemplative, reminiscent of the experience of watching the ocean or the sky. See her art at dianneromaine.com.

Christian Roman (page 157) is a story artist at Pixar Animation and has been in the animation industry for over 20 years. He has worked on such projects as *The Simpsons*, *King of the Hill*, *Disney's Fillmore!* and *Toy Story 3*. Some things about him can be learned at about.me/christianroman.

Cybele Rowe (page 159) was born in Sydney. She earned her BFA from The City Art Institute University of New South Wales before securing the oldest and largest gallery in Sydney and an award from the Australian Government enabling her to travel the world. Rowe moved to New York and showed paintings and sculptures at the Bergdorf Goodman Stores, The World Bank and Kennedy Center in Washington DC, and lectured at the Smithsonian Institute. When her son was born in 1998, Rowe and her family moved to the old mining town of Silverado in Southern California. Rowe's work is in the collections of Will and Jada Pinkett Smith, Halle Berry and EMI Records and in numerous public institutions such as the Australian Embassy, Washington DC; the World Trade Centre, Australia; and the Australian Consulate in New York. Read more at cybelerowe.com.

Janice Sandeen (page 205): "The road to 'who' is not a road, in my experience, but a continual arriving at a place that cannot be marked by an arrival or a departure. There can be telling 'about,' but even that is a facsimile, an exercise in looking at, or a momentary pause from What Is. 'About' is what can drop away again and again, which it has, and does over and over. Being, on the other hand, is the 'who,' which just is, and it is this Being that most informs the 'what' being written and shared here." —from contemplative fire: janicesandeen.wordpress.com.

Shiori Shimomura (pages 126, 143) was born in a suburb of Tokyo and began drawing on walls at around age two. She grew up wanting to be an artist, and found her way to Syracuse University where she studied illustration. She went on to study fashion illustration at the Fashion Institute of Technology and found work in the industry. Moving to San Francisco, she was between jobs and decided to try haircutting to tide her over, but she enjoyed the work and stuck with it. She now cuts hair at Barbarella Beauty Lounge in Berkeley, California, and continues to make art inspired by her travels.

Joyce Shon (page 35, 49) has been screen-printing for more than 40 years and has produced custom commercial work, images on fabric and fine art prints. She exhibits her work in the Bay Area.

Tony Speirs (page 113) was born in Washington State and grew up loving comics, cartoons, science fiction, nature and wildlife—and drawing. After stints as a silk-screen printer, sign painter, and freelance artist he attended the Academy of Art College in San Francisco, studying life drawing and illustration. Trips with his family to Mexico and Guatemala inspired a mythical, surrealistic direction in his paintings. Around 2000, Tony started adapting the style of fruit-crate labels in his paintings, combined with vintage pop-culture graphics as well as elements from other cultures. In 2008 Tony— with his wife and fellow artist, Lisa Beerntsen—founded Art Farm Motel, a collaborative group that produces and exhibits large-scale pieces. Tony has shown his paintings at galleries throughout the Bay Area, and his works have been featured on the covers of many publications and in books. He and Lisa live and paint in Sonoma County, California. See his art at tonyspeirs.com.

Bob Stang (pages 55, 199) paints. See his work at bobstang.com.

Livia Stein (page 27) studied history at UC Berkeley before going to India while working toward a Master's in South Asian Studies from the University of Pennsylvania. She studied photography at Art Center College in Los Angeles then shifted to painting and monotype while working on a Master's at San Francisco State University. Today, she lives and works in Oakland and is Professor of Art at Dominican University in San Rafael, California. Livia's art has been exhibited in Europe, South America, India and throughout the U.S. In 2007, she had a residency and solo show at the de Young Museum in San Francisco. She has also had residencies in India. Her work is in the Collection of the Achenbach Foundation for Graphic Arts, Oakland Museum of California, Dominican University, University of Iowa Art Museum and many others. Find her online at liviacstein.com.

Professor **Chip Sullivan** (page 201) has devoted his career to promoting landscape architecture as an art. His work illustrates the delicate balance between humans and nature and has been shown in galleries throughout the U.S., Canada, and Italy. Chip is the author of *Drawing the Landscape*, a popular treatise on drawing and the creative process, and the *Illustrated History of Landscape Design*, co-authored with Elizabeth Boults, among others. Since 2006, Chip has produced a series of comics for *Landscape Architecture Magazine* titled "Creative Learning." He was the 1985 Fellow in Landscape Architecture at the American Academy in Rome. Sullivan was the subject of a documentary titled "The Professor" by Emmy award-winning director Allan Holzman. He received his BLA and MURP from the University of Florida. Take a walk through gonzogardens.com.

Rachell Sumpter (page 117) grew up in the suburbs of San Francisco. Swayed and beguiled by nature, she travels the west coast of the U.S. to find inspiration. Sumpter's work has been exhibited worldwide, including Jack Hanley (San Francisco), Allston Skirt (Boston), Richard Heller (Los Angeles), Sunday L.E.S. (New York), The Orange County Museum of Art and the Los Angeles County Museum of Art. She has been written about in *The Boston Globe, San Francisco Chronicle, Mean, Giant Robot, ArtWeek, Artforum* and *McSweeney's Issue 24* among others. See her full-color artwork at rachellsumpter.com.

Kyle Trujillo (page 119) honed his skills at the Richmond Art Center as student and volunteer. His new work is more spiritual than physical art. He claims it's really great stuff.

Jon Turner (page 107) was born in Coggeshall, England and now lives in Manchester. A graduate of Balliol College, Oxford University, he likes books, biscuits, trees, sunshine, rock & roll, getting lost in strange places and drawing strange things. His illustrations and designs combine vintage imagery and a literary sensibility with a surreal sense of fun. More at thisisjonturner.com.

Kerry Vander Meer (pages 53, 129, 131) explores the natural world through painting, printmaking, performance and sculpture. Her art has been presented at museums, galleries, and universities worldwide and has won artist-in-residency awards at the Cill Rialaig Project in Ireland, Millay Colony in Upstate New York, Villa Montalvo in Santa Clara, California, and Foundation Valpariso in Spain. While in Ireland, Vander Meer designed a community project called Beir Mo Bheannache Chucu (Remember Me to Them) that brought together hundreds of people and involved the construction of over two hundred fabric and paper boats, each representing the families that migrated from the Iveragh Peninsula over the past 150 years. In California, Vander Meer sewed the boats together to form a large Celtic cross, which was exhibited at the Yerba Buena Center in San Francisco. Vander Meer taught art and yoga for 14 years at Creative Growth. She teaches monotype and mixed media workshops in Oakland and Mexico. More at kerryvandermeer.com.

Ben Walker (page 51) is a San Francisco-based illustrator but is mostly known for being the inventor of volcanoes. Check it out: benwalkerart.com.

Jerad Walker (pages 37, 73) is a multimedia artist who has been creating and showing nationally for more than 20 years. He believes art is a way of evolving, seeing, and sharing a journey that navigates the thread of imagination into manifestation. See his work at jeradwalker.com.

Matt Weatherford (page 89) is an engineer, fake movie critic and aspiring novelist. He lives near Denver, Colorado with his wife and son. The family enjoys hiking, camping, fishing and shoveling snow. Matt met Daniel Ari when they were both freshman in college and trying to learn how to make people laugh. He has written extensively about Las Vegas and the many opportunities it offers people to make regrettable mistakes. He hopes one day to have his unpublished works discovered in a desk drawer, and for people to declare him an unsung genius. Then he will jump out of the closet and say, "Ha! I'm not dead. Now you have to love me." You can read his humor writing at BigEmpire.com.

Wayne White (page 147) is an American artist, art director, illustrator, puppeteer, and more. Born and raised in Chattanooga, Wayne uses his memories of the South to create inspired works for film, television, and the fine art world. In 1986, Wayne became a designer for the television show *Pee-wee's Playhouse*, and his work was awarded three Emmys. After traveling to Los Angeles with his wife, artist Mimi Pond, Wayne designed sets and characters for television shows such as *Shining Time Station, Beakman's World, Riders In The Sky,* and *Bill & Willis*. He also worked in the music video industry, winning Billboard and MTV Music

Video Awards as an art director for The Smashing Pumpkins' "Tonight, Tonight" and Peter Gabriel's "Big Time." More recently, Wayne has had success as a fine artist with paintings featuring oversized, three-dimensional text painstakingly integrated into vintage landscape reproductions. Wayne White is the subject of the documentary *Beauty Is Embarrassing: The Wayne White Story*. You'll enjoy browsing at waynewhiteart.com.

Heather Wilcoxon (pages 101, 174, 195) was born in Los Angeles but has lived on the Sausalito Waterfront in Northern California for more than 30 years. Her home is a 100-year-old houseboat called the *Delta Queen*. By living in a unique and special community of artists, boat builders and maritime workers, she has been able to afford a studio close by that supports her art practice and career. Her figures capture both the comedy and tragedy of humanity in vibrant childlike imagery and symbols. She exhibits at the Jack Fischer Gallery in San Francisco and many other places. heatherwilcoxon.com.

Derek Wilson (page 115), born and raised in California's Bay Area, has been using his hands to make things since he can remember. The great grandson of a blacksmith, Derek's love of creating led him to the California College of Arts where he earned simultaneous BFAs in drawing and illustration. He currently teaches multimedia studies at the College of Marin; and in his spare time he cooks, brews beer, gardens, and makes functional art like cigar-box guitars, puppets and home improvements with attention to design.

INTRODUCING THE QUERON AND *ONE WAY TO ASK,* THE LONG VERSION

I created the form called *queron* as a right-shaped vessel for my poetic efflux. It matches the way my creative expression dances with my experience. And for me it's a sweet flight to imagine other poets who will be better at writing querons than I, poets who will use the queron's parameters and intentions to delve into the wonder of being human. I can't wait to read what they create; and in case *they* is *you,* here's the basic queron form for you to play with:

- Seventeen lines are grouped into three quintets and a final couplet.
- The rhyme scheme is ***ababa bcbca cdcdb dd***.
- Each line has the same number of syllables, or some other conscious intention informs line length.

I developed the queron in preparation for the November 2009 Poem-A-Day Challenge hosted by Robert Lee Brewer at Writersdigest.com. I saw the event as an opportunity to practice an original poetry form 30 times or more.

Key to the queron's development is my love of formal poetry. Many have written about the benefits of adding parameters to the processes of creativity across artistic media. For me it's about engaging the puzzle-solving, game-playing parts of my brain. I like playing with language like Lego blocks, choosing the right ones, finding new combinations. With formal poetry, I am able to arrive at a recognizably complete structure—not one that's beyond modification, but something that resembles what I set out to build: a poem.

Writing in form also serves to slow down my writing process, making each choice more deliberate and conscious. That's my natural approach in writing poetry, so writing in form supports my tendency toward deliberation. A typical queron draft usually takes me a day or two, and the poems in this book have matured and improved over the course of months to years. Many have been submitted to publications, some have been published, and others have been rejected half a dozen times or more, which has driven me to consider more changes. Here is a recent queron draft:

"Cartesian Reduction"

> *I am; therefore, I do…*
> *I do; therefore, I think…*
> *I live; therefore, I poop…*
> *I poop; therefore, I stink.*
> He sees the sky is blue;
>
> he leaves his pen and ink.
> He thinks and he paces.
> He's thirsty and he drinks.
> In his wardrobe, black capes
> to put on; therefore, to
>
> escape his own landscape.
> He moves through Amsterdam.
> His mind feels like a space
> wanting an epigram.
> *She grows quick as a wink;*
>
> *therefore, my dearest lamb,*
> *we will share this plum jam.*

This queron has six syllables in each of its seventeen lines. When I was developing the queron, a sonnet's fourteen lines felt too brief. I liked the length of John Berryman's 18-line dream songs. I was settling on three quintets when I hit on the final couplet and felt I had arrived.

As in all querons, the lines rhyme in these sets:

Lines 1, 3, 5 and 10 (do, poop, blue, to)

Lines 2, 4, 6, 8, and 15 (think, stink, ink, drinks, wink)

Lines 7, 9, 11, 13 (paces, capes, scape, space)

Lines 12, 14, 16, 17 (Amsterdam, epigram, lamb, jam)

As you can hear and see, I'm not attached to what poets call *true* or *perfect* rhyme. I'm more drawn to rhyme's variations like assonance (do/poop) and what poets call *near* or *imperfect* rhyme (ink/drinks). I also dig anagrams. To me, the visual, letter-level similarity of *paces, capes, scape,* and *space* register as a rhyme that's every bit as compelling and significant as true rhyme (*paces, faces, races, traces*).

Rhyme serves me like a stud wall. I use it to build the poem, to guide myself into new richness of meaning, and to have an indication about when the poem is drafted. But like studs, the rhymes don't need to remain obvious or visible—or even intact—for me to feel satisfied that they've done their job once the poem is drywalled and painted.

I came up with the term *associative harmony* to describe a palimpsest of rhyme edited out over multiple revisions. There could be associative harmony between the words *azure* and *truth*, for example, because the former is a type of blue and the latter is a form of *true*; and those words rhyme. *True* and *blue* may have been the words I used in the first draft and eventually changed. What's more, *azure* and *truth* are both five letters long with *u* as the third. It's about a subtle as rhyme can get and, in my opinion, just right.

Some of the poems in this book may have rhymes that have become so subtle as to be undetectable. Sometimes, for example, only an *f* sound links words—and one or more of those words may have been pushed back into the line or dropped to the next line so that the end-words are no longer even remotely tied. My opinion of rhyme is that it's a tool for the poet.

Anyway true rhymes at the ends of lines often make poems sound too sing-song for my tastes. What's worse is that you can't use the word *orange* if you're sticking to true

rhyme; whereas when you broaden your sense of rhyme, you can pair it with *range,*
hinged, anger, garage, forage, and hundreds of other words.

Getting back to "Cartesian Reduction," what you can't see on the page is the work
behind the poem, the *asking* involved. The first draft had more jokes. Poetry nerds
may have chuckled at lines like "I rhyme; therefore, iamb," and horticulturalists who
appreciate simultaneous references to Popeye and Hamlet might have appreciated
"Tuber, or not, I yam."

But the first draft didn't have any kind of narrative. It was only variations on Descartes'
cogito, "I think; therefore, I am," written only to demonstrate the rhyme scheme and syllable
count. But as I started to revise, I did light research into the life of Rene Descartes. I learned
that due to his station as a respected philosopher, Descartes wore black robes that signified
nobility. (I took the liberty of calling them *capes*.) I also found out that he spent much of his
life in Amsterdam and had a daughter with a servant woman. His daughter Francine was two
or three years old when Descartes published the *cogito*, but she died a few years later, breaking
Descartes' heart.

Though this last bit of research is absent from the words of the poem, I feel both
Francine's death and Descartes' imminent heartbreak in the poem. Having learned
of them, I can't help but feel them. And now that you know, you will have a different
relationship to the poem, too.

I confess to imagining an audience who either automatically knows what I'm talking
about or who takes the time to follow research trails that lead them there. But even
without an audience that shares an exact understanding, I believe that the craft in
a poem is apparent as a richer resonance, regardless of whether the meanings conveyed to
the reader are exactly the same as those the poet had in the front of her or his mind.

These thoughts feed into a central aspect of querons: they are for questions. I believe
poetry is an ideal medium for humans to engage the ephemeral, unanswered and
unanswerable. Influenced by Rilke's advice to "live the questions now," my experiments

in creating the queron came from wanting to find ways to support the way my mind uses poetry to express wonder, *to ask*.

Querons support the way my mind engages questions—which is what it does when I write poems. Searching out my rhymes—even rhymes nobody else can detect—and counting syllables slows me down to a state of greater, more attentive curiosity. At the same time, auditioning words more carefully makes me reach farther into the depths of language to find what I want to say. The words I recruit often bring their own connotations that can alter or deepen what I thought I was putting into the poem.

In querons, the stanza breaks create a sort of triptych, the final couplet either standing as a summary or wrapping into the third beat. These three parts are often three different perspectives on a topic. The stanza breaks are opportunities to delve under two more layers, to see the subject from two other viewpoints, or to admit two on-the-other-hands. The narrative possibilities are also rich, as the stanza breaks can make the poem into a miniature three-act play.

The name *queron* evolved from the root of query and querent (the one for whom a tarot reading is done). Initially, the recipe for queron was more overt and rigid about questioning. The requirement was that the first punctuated sentiment had to end in a question mark. I thought that querons would not have titles, but could be referred to by the opening question.

That turned out to be too prescriptive, so I decided to give querons titles and stipulate instead that a question mark should appear somewhere in the poem. But even that felt too limiting because the feeling of questioning isn't always expressed with a question mark. The statement, *I wonder how photosynthesis works*, ends in a period but still conveys a *sense* of questioning. What remained was that querons should have that sense of wonder, awe, unknowing, open-endedness, ephemerality, ineffability—and asking. And for me that was pretty much a given as I rarely write poems solid with certainty.

What I hope is that as other poets put their attention to this form, it will come to denote questioning. In other words, it will be enough that a poem is a queron to let the reader know to read the poem with a sense of wonder. Seeing three quintets and a couplet should affect the reader's understanding the way a final question mark or exclamation point would determine your understanding of the words *It was an accident.*

That's not an unreasonable hope for a poetry form. Seeing a haiku prepares a reader for nature imagery and a surprising juxtaposition. Seeing a limerick prepares a reader for broad or bawdy humor. For centuries, a set of fourteen lines was a clear indication that you were tucking into a sonnet; and thus, the subject would be love.

Poets, will you help me make 5+5+5+2 a combination that alerts readers to the fact that we are *asking*? (But let's not lead them to believe they'll always find a pat answer.)

The sonnet in recent times has been the subject of many experiments, and in my opinion it remains a rich form despite what William Carlos Williams famously said about crabs in boxes. Not wanting to wait for centuries to see how querons might be stretched and bent to fit around subjects, I have run my own experiments on the form to see what's essential about it and what is flexible. The rhyme scheme seems to be an important anchor throughout these variants, which fall into three main categories:

Experiments in line length. Querons have an intentional line length. Each line could have the same number of syllables—ten, twelve, two, or twenty-nine. But intentional line length could also mean that line one has one syllable, line two has two, and so on. Or it could mean that each line has the same number of accented syllables. Or words. There are many possibilities. My Frankenstein poem, "Meeting the Doctor," (page 156) intentionally does away with uniformity of line length in support of the theme and tone of the poem. "What Experiences" (page 204) has a line length based on words instead of syllables, and the pattern is the Fibonacci series. The first half of the poem counts up: 1, 1, 2, 3, 5, 8, 13, 21. The 34-word quote from Janice Sandeen is the middle line, and then the lines count back down again to one.

Experiments in poem length. The rhyme scheme telescopes. What I call "hyperqueron" extends the scheme to four or more quintets before the final couplet (***ababa bcbca cdcdb dxdxc xyxyd yy***). "Soham What I Am" (page 112) is an example. I also tried "demiqueron" which ends the poem at twelve lines (***ababa bcbca cc***), but I didn't include any samples of that experiment. I also started a screenplay in queron that grew to about 30 quintets before moving onto the backburner.

Experiments in format. In "Querons to Morpheus," (pages 136, 138), part two is a reflection of part one, an inverted queron that starts with the couplet. That pairing of querons also has lines whose syllables count up from one to seventeen in part one and back down from seventeen to one in part two.

I've also tried arranging the lines in a queron for music. Since quartets can be easier than quintets to set to music, I regrouped the seventeen lines as four quartets and a final line. I've also added refrains, choruses and backing vocals into some of these, like "Don't Forget It (With Curly Weaver)" (page 66). The queron form is pretty well hidden in that poem, but it does form an undeniable understructure.

One queron not in this collection came as a dialog between myself and a crab in a supermarket tank. It struck me that I could typeset the queron as a page from a screenplay with that form's textual furniture (INT – SUPERMARKET – DAY).

And then there's the art, a separate and equally gripping adventure for me. I was in the bath on a December night in 2012 when I felt the first inkling that it was time to select and publish the best of the querons I'd written, some 250 at the time. Before this project, I collaborated almost exclusively with Lauren Ari, an amazingly gutsy artist, and my wife. That night in the bath, it occurred to me how many artists I know. Thanks to Lauren and I both being artists, we are friends with a lot of them, so for this book, I decided to ask many people to contribute art. Collaborating with many artists has been like discovering a new planet in relation to earth. The art isn't part of the queron form, but to me the art introduces a mutual gravity with the poems.

With Lauren, I sometimes wrote poems to illustrate her drawings. Other times she made art to illustrate my poems. The collaborations in this book worked both ways as well. Many artists were inspired to create new artwork from the poems I sent them. That's how Derek Wilson, Roz Chast, Carole Ambauen, Livia Stein, Angelin Miller and Reza Farazmand worked, among others. Some artists contributed art they had already made. That's how I became the proverbial candy-store kid, poring through portfolios of art by Henrik Drescher, Wayne White, Heather Wilcoxon, Katina Huston, Kato Jaworski, R. Crumb, Chuck H. Alston and Gitty Duncan, looking for pieces to illustrate in words or to match with poems I had already drafted.

With some artists, I explored the spectrum between poem-first and art-first collaboration. For example, Tony Speirs often explores imagery from cartoons and popular culture in his paintings, so I specifically sent him my Popeye poem and a few others that would match his style. Christian Roman, a Pixar artist, expressed his interest in genre writing, so he was a good candidate to illustrate my contemporary take on the Frankenstein story. John Yoyogi Fortes' art has a dark, chaotic flavor, so I sent him dark, chaotic poems; and just when I thought I should give him a wider selection, he sent the perfect art for "Post-apocalypse for dummies."

In some cases, art and poem were created separately. For example, I wanted a vampire image for "Queron 18," and signed up Mark Hammermeister's Bela Lugosi portrait at Behance.com. One day on the train, I told a friend about my project, and he suggested I contact his friend Ben Walker. I've never meet Ben in person, but he was glad to share the cake topper he had drawn, and it clicked immediately with "We agree," a love poem I'd written to Lauren.

Janice Sandeen and I had a wonderfully synchronous collaboration, working back and forth between image, idea and words. We took time to discuss and clarify, rewrite and redraw. The poem kept changing; and her art kept changing. At times it became frustrating, but we learned to trust each other and push through. With her, I think, I went farthest in discovering what collaboration can be.

It was wonderfully fulfilling to work with my artist friends, and also wonderful to be in touch with artists I don't know personally but have long admired. When I was in my teens, for instance, I painted the word "Zippy" in big, bright, colorful spots—years before becoming a follower of Bill Griffith's syndicated comic *Zippy the Pinhead*. In my thirties, I found Bill Griffith's address and sent him the canvas. He drew his Zippy character onto my Zippy painting and sent it back. When I conceived of this book, he was near the top of my list of artists to approach. He said he remembered my canvas, and he sent an image of a Dingburg family for me to include in the book. I wrote the poem that goes with his image by imagining my own family in the scene.

It was similarly exciting to communicate with Roz Chast, Henrik Drescher, R. Crumb, Wayne White, Roberta Gregory, Stefan Bucher, Krystine Kryttre, and other well known artists. Though some artists I approached weren't able to contribute to this book (they'll be contacted regarding volume two), I was consistently delighted at how willing folks are, even those who eventually had to decline.

Corresponding with Tony Millionaire about his dark comic strip, *Maakies*, I said I liked how it was about persevering despite ridiculous hardship—external and self-inflicted. He said, "You really get *Maakies* more than most people." That was a gratifying thing to hear and made me thankful to have developed a poet's sensitivity.

Cover artist Eric Lindsey is a professional colleague of mine. I knew his style from the art he made on dry erase boards around the office. He is a formidable graphic designer with the latest digital tools at his fingertips, but I'm really glad to give him more opportunity to show his talent for hand rendering.

In seeking collaborators, I enjoyed ranging away from illustrators and visual artists alone. I'm happy to have work from glass artist Jay Musler, sculptor Cybele Rowe, screen-printer Joyce Shon, poet/artist Allan Peterson, jack of all trades Mark Bell, one-man rock band Andrew Goldfarb, and writers Marna Scooter Cascadia and Matt Weatherford, as well as my daughter, Mirabai, who at nine does everything.

What norm emerged across these artistic collaborations? Only that I asked artists if they wanted to play, and they said yes. If they said no, I asked if we might play another way, and then, sometimes, they said yes. From there, things unfolded and grew as they needed to with many surprises, changes and adaptations every step of the way. The improvisation of asking can be such a delightful necessity!

I truly hope you enjoy reading and looking. Reading slowly, out loud, and more than once are recommended approaches. I also encourage you to try your hand at writing queron. Follow your sense of wonder, and be willing to arrive at no answer, but more wonder. Give yourself permission to take your time and to test each word for its meanings and sounds. If you arrive at something you like, send it to me. My email is efflux@sonic.net, or you can comment at my blog, FightsWithPoems.blogspot.com or reach me through norfolkpress.com.

Daniel Ari
San Francisco, 2016

The following journals, anthologies and presses
have published poems and art that appear in this book:

Soul-Lit, Fall/Winter 2015
"Aleph"

Thema, Autumn 2015
"Feedback on 4.5"

Really System, Spring 2015
"Consider the machine"

Rio Grande Review, Issue 44, 2015
"We agree"
"Fortune's Castle"

Los Angeles Review of Los Angeles, June 2015
"Reasonable Doubt v. Abiding Conviction"

Edwin E. Smith Quarterly Magazine, Summer 2014 featured poet:
"No one moves"
"Vision quest vision"
"The rabbi's daughter"
"The inches between"
"House guest"
"Evening etude"
"Baba, an American woman"

NonBinary Review, September 2014, Mary Shelley's Frankenstein issue:
"Meeting the doctor" with art by Christian Roman (reprint)
October 2015, 1001 Arabian Nights issue:
"Class action suit: Women v. Shahryar"

Flapperhouse, Summer 2014
"What's cooking"
"The fallow months"

Gold Dust Magazine, December 2013
"Fairy panic" with art by Lauren Ari

carte blanche, Issue 19, Winter 2013
"Ways to this man's heart"

Cardinal Sins Journal, poetry contest winner, Fall 2013
"Misery Mojo and the Minds Less Blown"

Hobo Camp Review, Issue 18, Autumn 2013
"Who wept at the romance"

Wisdom Crieth Without, May 2013
"After the party" with art by Ann Sheng

Tales of the Undead—Suffer Eternal, Volume III, anthology by Horrified Press, 2013
"Meeting the doctor" with art by Christian Roman
"The Pale Man" with art by Eric Lindsey
"Queron 18" with art by Mark Hammermeister

Ugly Babies, anthology by James Ward Kirk Press, 2013
"Warts and all" with art by Angelin Miller
"Unearthly whiz" with art by Stefan G. Bucher

Turbulence, Issue 8, 2012
"Zombie movie climax"

Wild Age Press Anything Goes Contest, 2012 (honorable mention)
"Serious ink"

THANK YOU

Throughout this collaboration, gratitude has been as ubiquitous for me as air. Everyone: thank you.

Yes, you—thank you!

Thanks to the artists, each and all. Thanks to Derek Wilson, Stefan Bucher and Henrik Drescher for being on board early with encouragement and new ideas. Thanks to Janice Sandeen for bringing me beyond givens time and again. Thanks to the sensitive, intelligent and articulate people who shared their thoughts and feelings on working drafts: the poets Alison Luterman, Taylor Graham, Connie L. Peters, James B. Wheeler, Ed Aust, and Ina Roy-Faderman; the professional wordsmiths Anna Bartley, Janet Louise Patterson, Jeff Haggin, Matt Stafford, and Dave Higdon; and my parents Judy and Gerald Fleischmann.

Robert Lee Brewer re-sparked my poetic drive when I needed it. Allie Marini helped give my book a cohesive order. Stefan Bucher came back to put beauty into the design. Eric Lindsey rocked the cover. Paul McNees set my poems to music. Natasha Dennerstein gave me incredibly generous guidance in bringing this book into the world—leading me to Charles Cunningham who published it as a gorgeous, sensual volume that's a thrill to hold and peruse. Am I right?

I feel moved to thank Epsilon, my employer, for a creative livelihood that supports and fuels my creative life.

My friends Eric Dodds, Stephanie Keefer, Marna Scooter Cascadia, Terence Keane, Matt Weatherford and Steve Blumenthal have fanned my creative fires over the arc of my lifetime. And so, of course, has Lauren Ari, my life partner, Wonder Woman, who is with me through my best creative efforts, most especially our daughter, Mirabai.

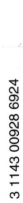